JESUS' THREE COMMUNION DECLARATIONS

From the Sacred Anointing Oil to the Precious Blood of Jesus

Jesus' Three Communion Declarations
From the Sacred Anointing Oil to the Precious Blood of Jesus

806, Seolleung-ro, Gangnam-gu,
Seoul, Republic of Korea 06014
http://www.tongbooks.com

copyrights © 2024 by Byoungho Zoh
All rights reserved

No part of this publication may
be reproduced or transmitted in any form or by
any means, electronic or mechanical, including
photocopying, recording or any information storage
or retrieval system, without permission in writing
from Byoungho Zoh or Tongdokwon.

Printed in South Korea

ISBN 979-11-90540-51-3 03230

JESUS' THREE COMMUNION DECLARATIONS

From the Sacred Anointing Oil to the Precious Blood of Jesus

Byoungho Zoh

tongdokwon

ENDORSEMENTS

🕊 Dr. Ronnie W. Floyd 🕊

Author, Speaker, Ministry Strategist, and Former President of the Southern Baptist Convention, the National Day of Prayer, and the Pastor Emeritus of Cross Church

Through the Global Church Network, I had the pleasure of meeting Dr. Byoungho Zoh. When I preached God's Word in one of their global gatherings in Manila, Philippines, I deeply sensed the Spirit of Jesus upon Dr. Zoh and everything he shared.

This made me aware of his extraordinary commitment to the Bible and the fulfillment of the Great Commission. His passionate zeal for Scripture and helping people to understand the Scriptures is genuine.

Believing the crucifixion of Jesus is the unified narrative of the Bible, which demonstrates how much God loves us and everyone across the globe. Over a decade ago, I led our multi-campus church in America to change our name to Cross Church. After reading his newest work, Jesus' Three Communion Declarations, I wanted to give a standing ovation for his deep commitment to the cross of Jesus Christ. When he writes about the Old Testament narrative leading "To the cross," the Four Gospels tell us the story of "The cross," and the Acts to the Epistles share with us the story, "From the cross," I wanted to shout! God loves us so much!

Thank you, Dr. Byoungho Zoh, for your love and passion for the Bible, Jesus Christ, our Lord and Savior, and the supernatural power of the Holy Spirit. God uses you to invest, inspire, and influence the Global Church! To God alone be the glory!

🕊 Dr. Leonard Sweet 🕊

Best-selling Author (most recently *The Sound of Light, Jesus Human, Designer Jesus*),
Professor (Drew University, George Fox University, Northwind Seminary)

Dr. Byoungho Zoh's Jesus' Three Communion Declarations offers a stunningly fresh perspective on communion and the connection between sacred anointing oil and Jesus' blood. By approaching the Bible as one cohesive narrative, Dr. Zoh uncovers insights that have long been hidden in plain sight, solidifying his reputation as one of the world's leading voices in biblical scholarship. A must-read for anyone seeking to deepen their grasp of biblical interconnections, intertextuality, and symbolism.

🕊 Dr. James O. Davis 🕊

Founder/President
Global Church Network, Global Church Divinity School

When I reflect on Dr. Byoungho Zoh and his latest book, 《Jesus' Three Communion Declarations : From The Sacred Anointing Oil To The Precious Blood of Jesus》, friendship, leadership and scholarship are at the front of my mind.

Through God's providence Dr. Zoh and I met for the first time in person at The Wittenberg 2017 Congress, in celebration of the 500th Anniversary of the Protestant Reformation. I am most grateful for our friendship that has been forged in faith with focus to finish the Great Commission.

In addition to friendship, his visionary leadership attracts the best of Christian leaders and inspires them to live their life on the heavenly level in Christ Jesus. His walk with the Creator is revealed through his information, inspiration and impartation. I always leave his presence a brighter person and better man.

Through his scholarship he has masterfully connected and communicated Jesus' Three Communion Declarations. In the so called modern era, we need to reminded of the wonderful working power in the blood of the Lamb. Just as the Israelites went out under the blood with a lamb on the inside, Dr. Zoh moves the reader from "then" to "now," and from remembering "the day of the Passover" to "remembering "the Lamb of God." He has written the quintessential book to renewing the reverence of the Lord's Supper and receiving its power in our lives. I highly recommend every Christian leader to purchase a box of Jesus' Three Communions and invest them into their congregants or/and their leadership team.

✍ Dr. Craig S. Keener ✍
F. M. and Ada Thompson Professor of Biblical Studies, Asbury Theological Seminary

As one would expect from Dr. Byoungho Zoh, 《Jesus' Three Communion Declarations : From The Sacred Anointing Oil To The Precious Blood of Jesus》 is immersed in Scripture. Dr. Zoh ably weaves together an important thread that runs through Scripture, from Passover to the Lord's Supper. In so doing he also points us to the climax of saving history, Jesus's death and resurrection on our behalf. He also connects the thread from God dwelling among Israel to the Spirit living in us. The Lord's Supper that we celebrate invites us to remember God's plan of salvation and empowerment for mission.

⚜ Dr. Yongkeun Kwon ⚜
Former President of Youngnam Theological University and Seminary

Dr. Byoungho Zoh delves deeply into a single theme of the Bible, demonstrating its interconnectedness with other themes and elucidating the pervasive mystery that permeates the entire biblical narrative. This is likely the result of his extensive reading and study of the Bible, which has led him to perceive the Bible as a unified narrative.

This time, Dr. Zoh addresses the question of sacraments. He posits that the sacraments are rooted in the symbolism of the 'priestly' covenant of the first Passover lamb and the sacrament of Jesus as the symbol of the new covenant of the 'kingdom of God.' He further suggests that this transition from the Old Testament to the blood of Jesus can be explained by the aforementioned symbolism. Furthermore, he elucidates that the new covenant of the sacraments encompasses the final Passover, the inaugural Eucharist, and the salvation and 'kingdom of God,' which reaches its zenith with the crucifixion.

The contemporary practice of the sacrament within the ecclesiastical context has resulted in a dilution of its formal aspects and a narrowing of its significance to the individual, thereby reducing the sense of its grandeur and its capacity to inspire. Accordingly, the author underscores the necessity for all churches to observe the sacrament of the Lord's Supper not merely 100 times, but in excess of 1,000 instances, and to do so with joy. It is therefore recommended that this book be read by pastors and church members alike, who may otherwise miss the excitement of life and the vision of the church through the sacraments received from the Lord (1 Corinthians 11:23).

≫ Dr. Gyeongjin Kim ≪
Senior Pastor of Somang Presbyterian Church,
Former Professor of Presbyterian University and Theological Seminary

One of the primary concerns of the Word-centered Reformed Church is the infrequent practice of the sacraments, particularly the Lord's Supper. It is a fortunate circumstance that the sacrament of the Lord's Supper has been restored to the Reformed Church in modern times. Furthermore, gratitude is owed to Dr. Zoh for his valuable contribution to the literature on the sacrament.

What is particularly noteworthy about Dr. Zoh's book is that he traces Jesus' sacramental practice to the Old Testament Passover. His innovative research elucidates the significance of the sacrament from its foundations in the pre-office of the kingdom of God to the interpretation of the blood of Jesus as God's salvific act.

As one reads down the pages, the significance of the sacraments is illuminated in a novel manner, akin to a comprehensive integration of disparate biblical passages. I enthusiastically endorse 《Jesus' Three Communion Declarations: From the Sacred Anointing Oil to the Precious Blood of Jesus》, to all believers and theologians; this helps us to gain a comprehensive understanding of God's salvation plan.

≫ Dr. Yeonhyun Kim ≪
Senior Pastor of Gurak Presbyterian Church, Doctor of Jurisprudence

Dr. Byoungho Zoh traces the meaning of the sacrament back to the Old Testament. By referencing the pivotal 'blood' in the ritual tradition of the Old Testament, particularly the Passover lamb's 'blood' (Exodus 12:13-14) during the Exodus and the Last Supper of Jesus in the New Testament, he underscores the interconnection between the Old and New Testaments.

The term 'Passover' signifies 'to pass over,' 'to leap over,' or 'to forgive' (life) (Exodus 12:13, 23, 27; Isaiah 31:5).

The New Testament's understanding of the Eucharist can be traced back to the Last Supper, which Jesus celebrated with his twelve disciples on the night before his death (Matt. 2; Mark 14; Luke 22; John 13). During this supper, Jesus distributed bread and wine as a symbol of his death and a precursor to his anticipated future celebration in heaven.

The earliest known reference to the Lord's Supper is found in Paul's writings in 1 Corinthians 11:23. In this passage, Paul asserts that the body and blood of Christ represent the sacrifice of his life as a new covenant of forgiveness. This is particularly aligned with the Gospel of John's assertion regarding the consumption of Christ's "flesh" and the ingestion of his "blood" (John 6:53-56).

In 《Jesus' Three Communion Declarations: From the Sacred Anointing Oil to the Precious Blood of Jesus》, Dr. Byoungho Zoh traces the origins of the sacrament back to the Old Testament. The 'blood' of the Passover in the Old Testament and the 'flesh and blood' of Jesus in the New Testament are not mere memories, symbols, or commemorations; rather, they are commands that imply human salvation as a contract between God and man and Jesus and humanity. Accordingly, this book, which elucidates the significance of the sacraments and the Old and New Testaments in a straightforward manner, will be greatly appreciated by numerous pastors, and we enthusiastically welcome its publication.

🕊 Dr. Younglae Kim 🕊
Professor of Methodist Theological University

In this work, Dr. Byoungho Zoh, a renowned author of the K-Bible, offers a comprehensive and insightful examination of the profound meaning and historical context of the Eucharist in 《Jesus' Three Communion Declarations : From The Sacred Anointing Oil To The Precious Blood of Jesus》. By focusing on the three declarations of Jesus in the Eucharist, this book offers a new perspective on the nature of faith and the essence of worship.

The initial chapter examines the profound significance of the 'new covenant' that Jesus proclaimed at the inaugural communion. In the Christian tradition, the bread and wine of the Eucharist symbolize the flesh and blood of Jesus Christ. Through this sacrament, Christians commemorate and express gratitude for Christ's atoning work on behalf of humanity. In a poignant manner, Dr. Byoungho Zoh elucidates how this pronouncement encapsulates the sacrifice and benevolence of Jesus.

The second declaration is that Jesus made the 'Christian'declaration during the first communion. This underscores the notion that Christians, in their union with Jesus, are entrusted with a mission as public servants within the kingdom of God. This serves to illustrate that the sacrament of communion is not merely a ritual; rather, it is a defining moment that marks the identity and mission of Christians.

The third declaration pertains to the presence of the Holy Spirit, also known as the Comforter. In the New Testament, Jesus promises that through the presence of the Holy Spirit, he will always be with his disciples. Dr. Byoungho Zoh provides a comprehensive analysis of the implications of the Holy Spirit's presence for the Church and Christians, elucidating the interconnection between the sacrament of communion and the work of the Holy Spirit. The presence of the Holy Spirit serves as a constant source of strength and encouragement for Christians on their spiritual journey.

Furthermore, it offers an integrated interpretation of the entire Bible as a unified narrative centered on the crucifixion of Jesus Christ. It offers insight into how God's plan of redemption was fulfilled through the Old Testament book of Exodus, the first Passover, and the first Eucharist in the New Testament. Dr. Zoh underscores the necessity of reading the 66 books of the Bible as a unified narrative, which serves to guide readers towards a more profound comprehension of the Bible.

Written with theological depth and spiritual insight, Dr. Byoungho Zoh's three Communion Declarations of Jesus makes a significant contribution to rethinking the nature and meaning of the Lord's Supper. Readers will emerge from this text with a reinvigorated appreciation for the Lord's Supper as the focal point of their faith, rather than merely a ritualistic observance. As a reminder of Jesus' sacrifice and love, and a call to a Christian life that lives out his teachings, this book is an invaluable asset that I highly recommend to people of all faiths.

Dr. Byoungho Zoh's Three Communion Declarations of Jesus represents a profound exploration of the Eucharist and the redemptive work of Jesus Christ. It will undoubtedly prove beneficial to all people of faith. It is my hope that this book will assist readers in recognizing that the Eucharist of Jesus is not merely a ritual, but rather a pivotal event within the framework of our faith. Dr. Byoungho Zoh's erudite analysis and profound insights will enrich your spiritual understanding.

❦ Rev. Hyoungbae Kim ❦

Senior Pastor of Seosan Evangelical Holiness Church,
Co-President of the Global Church Network (GCN) Seoul Hub

The Bible is the story of Jesus. The narrative of Jesus is concluded through the two pivotal events of the crucifixion and resurrection. It is through the sacraments that individuals may experience the reality of these events. Over the course of his career, Dr. Byoungho Zoh has established himself as a leading figure in biblical scholarship, with a particular focus on the Bible and its interpretation. He has made significant contributions to the field through his work on the 'Tong Bible' series and numerous other publications, which have helped to enhance our understanding of the Bible and foster familiarity with its contents. This book, entitled Jesus' Three Communion Declarations, represents an excellent contribution to theological literature, offering a profound and nuanced understanding of the sacraments and their practical implementation in pastoral contexts.

This book provides a comprehensive account of the continuity between the Old Testament 'Passover' and the 'Lord's Supper' of Jesus. It elucidates how the authority and power of Jesus' blood fulfills the narrative of God's salvation as depicted in the Old Testament.

The sacraments are of such significance that Jesus himself instructed his followers to "Do this in remembrance of me until I come again" (1 Corinthians 11:26). The book underscores that the sacrament of Holy Communion is not merely a recollection of the past; rather, it is a pivotal moment of covenant renewal with God, encompassing both the present and the future. It also highlights the pivotal role of the Holy Spirit in this sacrament. This will facilitate a more profound realization of our mission as Christians, as we experience the power of Jesus' sacrifice and resurrection with each Lord's Supper.

It is with great enthusiasm that I recommend this book to pastors and congregants alike, with the hope that it will facilitate a renewed understanding of the sacraments and elevate them from mere ritualistic observances to pivotal moments that enrich our spiritual lives. Jesus is the source and sustenance of life.

☙ Dr. Youngsang Noh ❧
President of Graduate School of Practical Theology

Dr. Zoh identifies three key declarations associated with the Christian sacrament: the declaration of the New Covenant, the declaration of Christianity, and the declaration of the presence of the Holy Spirit, also known as the Comforter. In the New Testament, the blood of the Passover lamb is identified as the blood of Jesus Christ, which is poured out in the sacrament (Luke 22:19-20). In this way, the sacrament places emphasis on the quickening effect of the blood of Christ.

Subsequently, Dr. Zoh elucidates that the flesh and blood of the Lord in the Lord's Supper is anointed with holy oil, the same oil that was used to anoint the priests in the Old Testament. Furthermore, he posits that through the New Testament sacrament of the Lord's Supper, we are bestowed with the status of a royal priesthood, a holy nation, and a kingdom. This royal priesthood and the associated calling as God's holy people inform the formation of Christian identity (1 Peter 2:9).

In conclusion, Dr. Zoh states that the Holy Spirit is received through the New Testament sacrament of communion. The anointing oil, which was used to anoint the priests in the Old Testament, and the blood of the Eucharist, which was also used in the Old Testament, are both sources of power. Through these sources of power, the Christian experience of the outpouring of the Holy Spirit is made possible (Acts 2:37-39).

Collectively, these three proclamations of the sacrament encapsulate the core tenets of the Christian gospel. The Lord's Supper bestows not only the forgiveness of sins but also the rebirth into the kingdom of God. I would like to extend my congratulations to Dr. Byoungho Zoh on the publication of his book, 《Jesus' Three Communion Declarations》, and I encourage all those with an interest in the subject to read it.

Dr. Sungkyu Park
President of Chongshin University

The key terms that have sustained Christianity for two millennia are 'Bible and Church.' However, if we break them down further, we find that they are 'New Covenant, Christians, and the Holy Spirit, the Comforter.' When these elements are combined, they form the concept of 'sacraments,' which serve as the cornerstones of the Christian tradition. Through these sacraments, Christians celebrate and experience the spiritual presence of Christ through the Holy Spirit.

By reading Dr. Zoh's book, 《Jesus' Three Communion Declarations》, readers can gain insight into the significance of communion within the context of the entire Bible. This understanding begins with the observation of the Old Testament priests' use of 'communion oil' and progresses to an examination of the biblical concept of communion. This concept can be defined as a genuine appreciation and celebration of Jesus' sacrifice and an experience of Christ's spiritual presence. It is my recommendation that this book be read with the intention of fostering a deeper spiritual connection with Christ and a stronger affirmation of faith.

Rev. Youngho Park

Former President of the Presbyterian Church in Korea,
Emeritus Pastor of Changwon Saesoon Church

The most significant symbols of Christian identity are baptism and the Lord's Supper. Baptism and the Lord's Supper are the only holy rites that Jesus instructed his apostles to perform. The Jewish religion maintains its identity through the observation of three major holidays: Passover, the Feast of Tabernacles (Pentecost), and Sukkot. Of these, Passover is considered the most significant. Of the fifteen steps observed by Jews during Passover, the fifth is designated as the Maggid, which is translated as "storytelling" in English. When the youngest child inquires about the rationale behind the consumption of unleavened bread on this particular night, the ingestion of bitter herbs, the practice of salting these herbs twice, or the requirement to sit in a reclined position, the father, the head of the household, is prepared to provide an explanation. For those seeking guidance on discussing baptism and the Lord's Supper, Dr. Byoungho Zoh's 《Jesus' Three Communion Declarations》 is an invaluable resource.

In order for it to be effective, it must be simple and enjoyable. For an extended period, I have endeavored to comprehend the significance of the Lord's Supper through the examination of theological literature, a pursuit that has proven to be challenging. When Martin Luther, Huldrych Zwingli, and John Calvin, who initiated and concluded the Protestant Reformation, convened to discuss the theological significance of the Lord's Supper, their perspectives were multifaceted. Protestant churches are divided into numerous denominations based on differing interpretations of baptism and the Lord's Supper. However, Dr. Byoungho Zoh's 《Jesus' Three Communion Declarations》 provides a comprehensive and accessible introduction to the Bible's teachings on these topics, offering insights that are both informative and engaging.

A considerable period of time has elapsed since the Church has demanded a new Reformation. The path forward is clear: members of the Church must be properly baptized, the experience of salvation must be restored through proper communion, and the entire Church must dedicate itself to fulfilling Christ's Great Commission in the full presence of the Holy Spirit. It is imperative that the atmosphere surrounding the Eucharist cease to evoke that of a funeral. Similarly, Hezekiah and Josiah sought to reinstate the Passover, which had been forgotten by previous generations, in order to restore faith in a kingdom of priests. It can be argued that a similar approach is required in order to restore faith in the kingdom of God in which we live, namely, that the Lord's Supper should be celebrated often and rightly. It seems reasonable to posit that Dr. Byoungho Zoh's 《Jesus' Three Communion Declarations》 will prove an inspiring and thought-provoking read.

☙ Dr. Kichun So ❧

Director of Jesus Sayings Hub,
Emeritus Professor of Presbyterian University and Theological Seminary

It is uncommon to encounter an individual who evinces such profound devotion to the Bible and to the teachings of Jesus as this author does. It is encouraging to observe an author who has produced a substantial body of work to be so enthusiastic about the same topic with a passion that resembles an exceptional heat wave.

In Japan, the hymn "Our Savior Who Bore Our Sins" is sung at both weddings and funerals. This is due to the fact that it is the sole hymn with which they are familiar. The author's initial exposure to hymnody occurred at the age of 11, when he sang "Nothing but the Blood of Jesus" without fully comprehending its meaning. He is now a world-renowned author who sings "Nothing but the Blood of Jesus" in English. This unwavering passion and fervor for the blood of Jesus serves as the primary motivating force behind the composition of this book. This passion is what ignites the enthusiasm and elation associated with the Lord's Supper, a quality that is currently lacking in many contemporary Christian congregations.

A lifelong storyteller who approaches the Bible as a narrative is now regarded as one of the world's leading exponents of the figure of Jesus. This book provides a comprehensive narrative of the Passover in Exodus and the Lord's Supper in the four Gospels, elucidating the interconnectivity between them through a storytelling approach. This enables a holistic reading of the Old and New Testaments. The Lord's Supper represents the sacrifice of the blood of the cross, which Jesus shed on a single occasion, thereby superseding the blood of the lamb at the conclusion of the Passover. From this point forward, the Passover, which had been celebrated by the Israelites in Canaan for generations, was replaced by the blood of Jesus and transformed from the sacred anointing oil to the precious blood of the cross.

If the blood of the lamb in Exodus was the means of salvation for the firstborn of Israel, then the final Passover of Jesus represents the remarkable power of his sacrifice to save the entire people from sin and death. In this manner, the author enthusiastically asserts that Jesus became the Passover lamb. While the Israelites adhere to the traditional covenant, which stipulates the use of a specific anointing oil composed of five ingredients (myrrh, broiler, iris, cinnamon, and frankincense oil) reserved exclusively for priests, Jesus, who replaced the oil with his own blood, extends an invitation to all to become priests and participate in the blood of the cross by coming directly to Jesus.

However, the narrative does not solely focus on the Eucharist scene. Instead, the author employs a creative approach, drawing the reader into the narrative of the Lord's Supper. The Israelites, who departed from the Exodus by hastily consuming unleavened bread and applying the blood of a lamb to the doorposts, are now invited to the final Passover supper, which celebrates the flesh and blood of Jesus. Although the tradition of celebrating the Passover still involves the consumption of unleavened bread and the use of the blood of animals, Jesus replaces these elements with his own flesh and blood, torn from the cross, and calls upon sinners to "remember me." The author puts forth a novel perspective, suggesting that while the Passover celebration marks the advent of the law, the Lord's Supper inaugurates the sacraments.

The celebration of Passover serves to reinforce the identity of the Jewish people, whereas the celebration of the Lord's Supper in memory of Jesus reinforces the identity of Christians. The Holy Spirit did not play a role in the Passover; however, the powerful presence and work of the Holy Spirit, also known as the Comforter, occurred at the Lord's Supper in memory of Jesus. While the work of the Holy Spirit is often studied with reference to the Pentecostal outpouring, the author suggests that the true work of the Holy Spirit begins with the Lord's Supper.

It is this author's recommendation that the book be read by anyone who has lost the sense of awe and reverence that should accompany the Lord's Supper. The author characterizes the Lord's Supper as the most comprehensive treatise on grace ever written. In recalling Jesus' command to "Remember me" during the Lord's Supper, Christians are imbued with the Holy Spirit, thereby fulfilling Jesus' Great Commission. In opposition to those who have lost the capacity for grace and are preoccupied with self-promotion, the author offers the prospect that when we experience the excitement of celebrating the flesh and blood of Jesus, we are restored to our role as evangelists, preaching Jesus alone.

᪲ Dr. Youngkyun Shin ᪲

Adjunct Professor of Youngnam Theological University and Seminary,
Doctor of Public Administration

I would like to extend my congratulations to Dr. Byoungho Zoh, a world-renowned authority on biblical interpretation known as "Dr. Tong," on the release of his new book. 《Jesus' Three Communion Proclamations: From the Sacred Anointing Oil to the Precious Blood of Jesus》 is an evangelical work that identifies the fundamental tenets of Christian faith in the Eucharist and applies them to the Christian life.

Dr. Zoh begins by acknowledging that the crux of his thousands of Bible readings is the blood of Jesus Christ. In a time when many people are polluting the faith with distorted ideas such as blessings, healing, tongues, and benedictions, I am deeply grateful that Dr. Zoh has shown us the way to a healthy Christian life by presenting the truth of the Bible, which he has experienced firsthand.

This book elevates the meaning of Passover to Jesus' proclamation of the Lord's Supper, guiding the reader through the significance and practice of the Lord's Supper in the present era and into the eternal eucharistic community of God's kingdom. It reaffirms our identity with Jesus' proclamation of the Lord's Supper, particularly in light of its announcement of the new covenant, and guides us to the core of the gospel.

The author introduces the Lord's Supper as Jesus' declaration of the presence of the Comforter, the Holy Spirit, and encourages readers to manifest the efficacy of the Spirit-filled Lord's Supper in their daily lives. In doing so, they present a holistic spirit of faith that transforms the institutional faith of the Old Testament into the empowering faith of today, the faith of the Passover into the faith of Jesus Christ, and legalistic faith into Spirit-filled faith.

I unreservedly recommend this book, which is not merely a volume of literature, but an invaluable spiritual guide that engages readers with the three declarations of the Lord's Supper and provides renewed strength and courage to live as citizens of God.

ᛞ Dr. Seungoh Ahn ᛞ
Professor of Youngnam Theological University and Seminary,
President of Global Missionary Institute

For over two millennia, the Church has observed the sacrament of the Lord's Supper, which Jesus instituted and commanded. Nevertheless, there has been a tendency to overlook the fact that the Lord's Supper is a memorial service that culminates in the Great Commission. In this book, Dr. Byoungho Zoh elucidates the significance of the Lord's Supper by examining the interconnection between the Lord's Supper and the believer's public office (that of a worker in the kingdom of God). By examining the three proclamations made by Jesus during the Lord's Supper—namely, the declaration of the new covenant, the declaration of Christian identity, and the declaration of the presence of the Holy Spirit, also known as the Comforter—Dr. Zoh elucidates the identity of the saints as witnesses to the kingdom of God. He underscores the necessity of continually reiterating and practicing this identity through the Lord's Supper.

In conducting this analysis, Dr. Byoungho Zoh, the author of this book, does not merely examine the New Testament; rather, he elucidates the significance of the Lord's Supper through a comprehensive intertextual approach that encompasses both the Old and New Testaments. In particular, he provides a detailed analysis of the significance of the Passover, the role of the lamb sacrificed during this event, the function of public servants as workers in the kingdom of God as depicted in the Old Testament, and the anointing oil utilized in rituals described in this religious text. He establishes a correlation between the ministry of Jesus and the identity of the saints who followed him. Additionally, the book incorporates a multitude of diagrams and classical iconography, which serve to illustrate the biblical text and facilitate comprehension of its core tenets.

This book will facilitate a more profound comprehension of the Old Testament for readers, enabling them to grasp the profound spiritual significance underlying the seemingly intricate Passover rituals, sacrifices, and priesthood. Furthermore, readers will gain insight into the interconnectivity between these elements and their relevance to the ministry of Jesus, as well as to the mission of believers. This book is essential reading for all believers, as it enables readers to perceive the divine act of salvation as revealed in the Old and New Testaments, and to comprehend the significance of the sacrament and its position within the broader context of salvation.

⌘ Dr. Sungmin Lee ⌘

Senior Pastor of Gangnam Sung Eun Church,
former professor at Methodist Theological Seminary

The ongoing pandemic has compelled churches and Christians to reflect on the core tenets of their faith. The question of the purpose of worship and the extent to which contemporary forms of worship may be perceived as lacking in substance remains a topic of ongoing debate.

In his book, 《Jesus' Three Communion Declarations》, Dr. Byoungho Zoh endeavors to address these questions. The Passover sacrifice constituted the focal point of Old Testament worship, while the Eucharist represents the central act of worship in the New Testament. These two rituals are inextricably linked in both historical and theological contexts.

At the Last Supper, Jesus celebrated the first sacrament of communion with his disciples, commemorating the sacrifice of his body and blood. He became the Passover Lamb for the entire world, thereby paving the way for those who believe in him to receive forgiveness of sins and gain entry into the eternal kingdom of God.

It is my hope that this book will serve as a source of inspiration and guidance for those seeking spiritual nourishment amidst the challenges of the ongoing pandemic. I hope that it will provide a refreshing perspective on worship and eternal life, drawing inspiration from the teachings of Jesus on the Eucharist.

❦ Rev. Sunghee Lee ❧

Former Superintendent of the Presbyterian Church of Korea (PCK),
Emeritus Pastor of Youndong Presbyterian Church

Protestant churches designate baptism and the Lord's Supper as sacraments. Such rites are designated as "holy" due to their divine origin, as ordained by Christ himself. Protestant churches place a premium on the use of the spoken word as a means of fostering a sense of community. The Catholic Church placed a premium on the sacraments, establishing them as the cornerstone of its institutional structure. Protestants adhere to the conviction that the sacraments derive their origin from the Word. A sacrament that is not in alignment with the Word cannot be considered to originate from Christ.

The sacrament of the Eucharist does not consist of bread and wine, as is commonly believed; rather, it is the body and blood of Christ. Consequently, the practice of the sacrament is not the sharing of bread and wine, but rather the sharing of the body and blood. Those who partake of the sacrament do so in commemoration of the sacrifice of Christ, sharing in the body and blood of the Son of God.

In his work, 《Jesus' Three Communion Declarations》 Dr. Byoungho Zoh reinterprets an established sacrament, employing novel terminology to facilitate a deeper understanding of the communion ritual. In particular, he traces the origin of the sacrament to the forgiveness of sins in the blood of the Passover and elucidates the true meaning of the sacrament in the miracles and parables of the New Testament. In this book, Dr. Byoungho Zoh provides an exhaustive examination of the sacraments as elucidated in the Scriptures. It is my recommendation that the book be given two thumbs up for its comprehensive yet accessible explanation of one of the two most important sacraments.

☙ Rev. Jinkoo Lee ❧
Senior Pastor of Sungru Presbyterian Church,
Member of the Global Church Network (GCN) Seoul Hub

I would like to extend my sincerest congratulations to Dr. Byoungho Zoh, a spiritual master who is pleasing in the eyes and heart of God. Dr. Zoh has illuminated the world with the teachings of the Bible, and he is driven by a sense of mission that compels him to share the best of Korea and abroad with regard to the Bible.

In the final Passover, Jesus conducted the inaugural "first communion" with "bread and wine," a tangible representation of Jesus' flesh and blood. He instructed his followers to commemorate his death through the consumption of communion with "bread and wine." As one of the authors of the book asserts, the lessons it imparts are of immeasurable and inexpressible spiritual value.

In this book, Dr. Byoungho Zoh demonstrates that the significance of the sacrament is that the blood of the final Passover lamb in the Old Testament is identified in the New Testament as the blood of Jesus Christ, which was shed during the sacrament (Luke 22:19-20). At the point of transition from the sacred oil to blood, Jesus proclaims a notable new covenant, shifting from "remember this day" to "remember me." At the final Passover of the Old Testament and the inaugural Eucharist of the New Testament, Jesus introduces the coming of the Holy Spirit, which serves to unify and connect Christians with Jesus as a public servant of the kingdom of God. It is my hope that through this book, you will be among those who experience the blessings of the Lord's Supper and recognize the veracity of the author's assertion that "Communion is good 100 times, and even better 1,000 times."

≈ Dr. Kyungchul Cho ≈
Emeritus Professor of Methodist Theological University

Dr. Byoungho Zoh, also known as 'Dr. Tong', has released a significant work on sacraments. The book focuses on the concept of "sacrament" as a pivotal idea and language that pervades the Old Testament in its connection to the Passover and the priestly nation. Consequently, it also traverses the entirety of the New Testament.

The Old and New Testaments have previously been read together in terms of concepts such as "covenant" and "salvation." However, this time the focus is on "sacrament," which is a more logical choice given that sacrament is not only the language of the Bible but also the core of our faith life. It is still repeatedly celebrated in the church to remind us of our saving grace. This book serves as an invaluable resource for elucidating the pivotal terminology that bridges the Old Testament, the New Testament, and the contemporary ecclesiastical context.

It is my sincere hope that this book will prove an invaluable resource for those seeking to gain a deeper understanding of the biblical meaning of the sacraments and to celebrate them in accordance with that meaning.

Dr. Heungjin Choi
President of Honam Theological University and Seminary

The book is a valuable contribution to the field, providing a comprehensive examination of the meaning and importance of the sacraments. It is anticipated that this text will prove invaluable in reinvigorating the faith of the Korean Church. I sincerely extend my gratitude.

contents

Testimonials

prologue

CHAPTER 1

From the Sacred Anointing Oil to the Precious Blood of Jesus

1. The First Passover, celebrated for 1,500 years
2. Passover Lamb, Offerings, and Public Servant
3. Anointing Oil and Blood: The Way to Forgiveness of Sins

CHAPTER 2

Jesus' Holy Communion Declaration

1. During the First Communion, Jesus Declared the "New Covenant"
   - The New Covenant established through the flesh and blood of Jesus
   - Symbolism of the Bread and Wine – Christian Communion
   - From "Celebrate this Day" to "Celebrate Me"

2. During the First Communion, Jesus made the "Christian" Declaration
   - The Parable of the Vine – Christians unified with Jesus
   - Christians – Public Servants of the kingdom of God
   - Christians – Whatever you desire

3. During the First Communion, Jesus declared the coming of the "Holy Spirit"
   - Immanuel through the Holy Spirit
   - When and Where the Holy Spirit will reside
   - The Role of the Holy Spirit

epilogue – The Communion as a Mission of the Great Commission

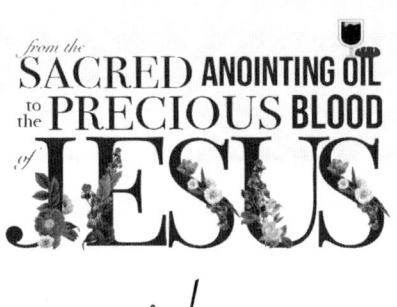

from the SACRED ANOINTING OIL *to the* PRECIOUS BLOOD *of* JESUS

prologue

My initial experience of a church service occurred at the age of 11. During this occasion, I was introduced to three key elements: prayer, hymns, and a sermon. During one of the hymns, I encountered a lyric that I was unable to comprehend. "The blood of Jesus is the sole means of atoning for my sins." The hymn struck me as somewhat incongruous. I was aware that if I had committed an offense against another individual, I could approach them, acknowledge my mistake, express remorse, and request pardon. If they accepted my apology and indicated their willingness to forgive, I would be forgiven. However, I lacked comprehension regarding the nature of this forgiveness and the role of the blood of Jesus in atoning for my transgressions. I was struck by the peculiar nature of the song. At that juncture, I was compelled to inquire, "What kind of song is this?"

After reading the Bible on numerous occasions, I have developed a preference for certain hymns. If I were to select three favorites, "There's Nothing But the Blood of Jesus to Wash Away My Sins" would be among them. The lyrics of the hymn are repeated with great frequency, with the refrain "There's nothing but the blood of Jesus to wash away my sins" occurring with notable regularity.

The assertion is made that the blood of Jesus is the sole means of atonement for sins.
The doctrine of the atonement asserts that the blood of Jesus is the sole means of cleansing from sin.
I am gratified by your assertion.

The Lord's Supper is inextricably linked to the blood of Jesus, which serves as a means of cleansing and forgiveness for sins. The Lord's Supper, the final Passover celebration shared by Jesus with his disciples on the night preceding his arrest, represents the inaugural event in this series of commemorations. In Luke 22:15, Jesus states, "I have eagerly desired to eat this Passover with you." He then proceeds to initiate the meal by offering a prayer of thanksgiving and breaking the bread, declaring, "This is my body." "This cup is the new covenant in my blood, which is poured out for you." (Luke 22:19-20).

After he had eaten, he did the same with the cup, saying, "Do this in remembrance of me." However, at the Passover celebrated one year prior and two years prior, when he was with his disciples, he did not instruct them to "eat the body of Jesus, drink the blood." Similarly, when he broke the barley loaves and fish for the multitudes in the field of Bethsaida and gave thanks and then gave them to them to eat, he did not say, "This is my body." He simply provided them with sustenance because he felt sorry for them and wanted to ensure they would not go home hungry.

However, on this occasion, the words were uttered with a distinct difference: "Take, eat, this is my body." In a manner analogous to the consumption of the lamb's flesh at the inaugural Passover in Egypt 1,500 years prior, Jesus' body was to be consumed. "Drink this," he said, "for this is my blood of the covenant." The blood of the Passover had always been "applied," but now it was "drunk." This was a highly significant pronouncement. In making this reference, Jesus was alluding to the "new covenant" that was established through the shedding of his blood, which was done once for all in the Holy of Holies on the cross.

Furthermore, Jesus linked the new covenant with the kingdom of God. Passover was a priestly holiday, and he connected it to the kingdom of God, stating, "For I tell you, I will not eat it again until it finds fulfillment in the kingdom of God" (Luke 22:16). He then proceeded to say, "For I tell you I will not drink again from the fruit of the vine until the kingdom of God comes" (Luke 22:18), further linking it to the kingdom of God. This is the new covenant, and it is to be celebrated.

In his discourse on the new covenant, Jesus informed those present that, as his Father had entrusted the kingdom to him, he had similarly bestowed upon them the privilege of being part of his kingdom, whether it be to partake of the sacrament or to assume a position of authority over the twelve tribes of Israel (Luke 22:29-30). The twelve tribes of Israel constituted a kingdom of priests 1,500 years ago. The notion of ruling over the twelve tribes was a radical proclamation that Jesus would occupy that throne and preside over the entire world.

To comprehend the term "messiah," it is essential to recognize that God has bestowed the kingdom upon Jesus. In the context of Christianity, the name "Jesus" is understood to signify the role of Savior. In his role as Savior, Jesus is the Christ, or Messiah, which can be defined as "an officer, an anointed one." In other words, Jesus was tasked with the responsibility of saving sinners due to his status as an anointed individual, or in other words, an officer.

There are three principal offices of public authority in the 'kingdom' that God anoints. These are the offices of high priest, king, and prophet. Collectively, these offices are referred to as the Christ, or Messiah. The three offices were bestowed upon Jesus of Nazareth by God. He bestowed the 'kingdom' upon him, and Jesus responded, "I will bestow the kingdom upon you." Subsequently, the apostle John came to understand this concept and articulated it in the Book of Revelation: "and has made us to be a kingdom and priests to serve his God and Father—to him be glory and power for ever and ever! Amen" (Revelation 1:6).

The perpetuation of the system of the kingdom of God is contingent upon the completion of the "kingdom" that God had entrusted to Jesus Christ. This completion was achieved through Christ's dedication, after which the kingdom of God's offices were entrusted to his disciples. In turn, the disciples fulfilled the mission of the kingdom of God's offices, and the dedication of the kingdom of God's officers continued for 2,000 years. It is for this reason that Christians experience joy in serving the Kingdom of God in their respective offices.

In his capacity as Creator, God fashioned a multitude of entities that are perceptible to the human eye, including the biosphere in which we, as creatures, reside. However, God's essence has been revealed to us in the form of the Word. Moses was able to perceive the words of God with remarkable clarity and vividness, and he conveyed them to the people. However, he did not have a direct visual encounter with God; he only caught a fleeting glimpse of God's back as God permitted him to do so. In conclusion, God's presence to His creatures was manifested in the form of the Word. It is through the extraordinary grace of God that He has bestowed upon us, His creatures, the gift of the Word in our lives. In his writings, the apostle John testifies to the arrival on earth of Jesus, who is regarded as a saint. John states that "the Word became flesh and dwelt among us" (John 1:14).

The expression of God's word of grace manifests in two distinct forms during the time of Jesus, as documented in the four gospels. The term "invisible word" is used to describe the written word of God. In addition to the Sermon on the Mount and the New Testament, numerous other writings from the Old Testament may be considered the "invisible word." The Bible, in its written form, represents the word of God and is centered on the figure of Jesus. The "visible word," as defined by Christian doctrine, refers to the sacraments established by Jesus Christ. These include the sacraments of baptism and the Lord's Supper. The "kingdom of God" on earth has been perpetuated by God through the sacraments of baptism and the Lord's Supper.

At the outset of his public ministry, Jesus underwent a baptism with water at the hands of John the Baptist. However, the practice of

Baptism of Christ | Piero della Francesca 作

baptism did not conclude with Jesus. Jesus ensured the continuation of baptism on Earth by instructing his disciples to "Therefore go and make disciples of all nations, baptizing them in the name of the Father and of the Son and of the Holy Spirit" (Matthew 28:19). Jesus transformed the "visible word," or "water," into the sacrament of baptism.

The term 'baptism' encompasses a range of meanings, including 'washing,' 'cleansing,' and 'anointing.' Those who profess faith in Jesus Christ as their Savior are baptized through the immersion of their bodies in water or the sprinkling of water on their heads. In baptism, sins are forgiven and the individual is united with Jesus, thereby receiving new life in a manner analogous to his resurrection. Furthermore, baptism is a symbolic ritual that serves as the official rite of initiation into Christianity.

In the New Testament, the baptism of John was not merely a cleansing ritual. John's baptism was accompanied by repentance, signifying acceptance of the forthcoming Messiah. Jesus commenced his public ministry with a baptism by the prophet John the Baptist in the Jordan River. This baptism marked the commencement of Jesus' ministry as "Christ the Messiah." The culmination of Jesus' public ministry was the crucifixion and subsequent resurrection. Jesus' baptism revealed him to be the Son of God and the Lamb of God, who made the once-for-all sacrifice on the cross.

Furthermore, the presence of the Father, Son, and Holy Spirit at Jesus' baptism, particularly the arrival of the Holy Spirit promptly following his baptism, substantiates the veracity of Christian baptism with water and the Holy Spirit. The baptism of Jesus was a pivotal event that set the stage for his ultimate sacrifice on the cross. Jesus' mission of salvation was accomplished through his crucifixion and subsequent resurrection, thereby fulfilling the prophecies associated with his name, which translates to "Savior." Those who believe in him are made children of God, and this profound belief is expressed through the sacrament of baptism.

In the early Christian church, baptism was regarded as an act of repentance and a profession of faith in Jesus Christ as Savior. Accordingly, baptism was conducted "in the name of Jesus Christ" (Acts 2:38) and "in the name of the Father, and of the Son, and of the Holy Spirit" (Matthew 28:19). The Apostle Paul instructed the members of the Roman church in the practice of baptism, providing them with a comprehensive account of Jesus's life and teachings. In baptism, Paul teaches that the individual is buried with their former self and, on the basis of Jesus' death, is born again and shares in His resurrection (Romans 6:3-7). This new birth allows the individual to live with Christ and become a member of His body, the church community (1 Corinthians 12:27). Paul's teachings continue to serve as a guiding force in the present era.

The sacraments are the rituals that commemorate Jesus' crucifixion mission. Therefore, baptism and the Lord's Supper are considered to be inextricably linked, serving to commemorate the ultimate mission of Jesus Christ, namely, the mission of the Lord's death. In other words, one may say that the Christian life is lived as a follower of Jesus through his public ministry, baptism, and the Lord's Supper. The sacraments facilitate our experience of God by uniting the "visible word" of baptism and the Lord's Supper. The path of life as exemplified by Jesus is learned through the sacraments, beginning with baptism.

A sacrament is a sacred rite observed in the Christian tradition that serves to convey the invisible grace of God through a visible conduit. The term "sacrament" is derived from the Latin word "sacramentum," which is derived from the Greek word "musterion." The latter term is defined as "secret, mystery," among other things. The term "sacrament" was originally translated by the ancient Church Fathers as "mystery." This was done because they felt that using the term "mystery" as the name of a rite, as in "he made known to us the mystery of his will according to his good pleasure, which he purposed in Christ" (Ephesians 1:9) and "the mystery that has been kept hidden for ages and generations, but is now disclosed to the Lord's people" (Colossians 1:26), would not adequately capture the meaning of a significant and sacred rite.

In The Institutes of Christianity, Calvin posited that baptism represents the 'initiation of faith' through which individuals are admitted to the church and grafted into Jesus Christ, thereby becoming recognized as children of God. He further suggested that the sacraments serve as a form of 'continual nourishment,' providing spiritual sustenance to those who have been initiated into the Christian faith. Baptism is thus a profound rite of passage, whereby an individual confesses their salvation from sin. It is a singular event, marking the commencement of one's Christian journey. Baptism is not repeated, but the sacrament of the Lord's death is celebrated on numerous occasions, either 100 times or 1,000 times. The death of Jesus, who offered himself as a sacrifice on the cross to save us from our sins, is celebrated repeatedly in the sacrament. The sacrament of communion, which celebrates the atonement made by Jesus through his death and resurrection, is not a singular event; rather, it is a sacrament to be celebrated repeatedly. In other words, the sacraments are intended to be repeated as a means of nurturing faith.

It is not uncommon for individuals to experience a sense of monotony when they engage in the same activity on numerous occasions. However, the adage "the more you do it, the better" suggests that the more frequently an action is performed, the more profound the experience becomes. This is why baptism is sufficient on a single occasion, whereas the sacrament of the Lord's Supper necessitates repeated participation. One may ensure the sacrament of the Lord's Supper is not perceived as tedious but rather as a source of inspiration and joy by engaging with the Bible. Through repeated reading and study of the Bible, individuals can gain a deeper understanding of the significance of the Lord's Supper, leading to a sense of gratitude and joy each time they partake. It is imperative for Christians to engage in the celebration of the Lord's Supper on a regular basis, and to recall the pronouncements made by Jesus at the inaugural communion.

In the final Passover, Jesus conducted the inaugural communion with bread and wine, representing his flesh and blood. He instructed his followers to commemorate his death by partaking in communion with bread and wine. This book will examine the three declarations made by Jesus at the first communion, with a particular emphasis on the sacrament that should be observed repeatedly. The first is the New Covenant declaration, the second is the Christian declaration, and the third is the declaration of the presence of the Holy Spirit, also known as the Comforter.

Subsequent to the three declarations of communion is the single offering of the cross of Jesus. A temporal interval exists between the three declarations of communion and the cross; nevertheless, the two are inextricably linked. This represents the transition from the use of sacred anointing oil to the application of the precious blood of Jesus. The transition from the anointing oil to the Precious Blood is not a continuation of the former as a different form; it is not that the anointing oil continues and the Precious Blood is used. Rather, it is that the anointing oil has ended and is now transformed into the Precious Blood, which persists as the Precious Blood. It is hoped that this excitement will always be present.

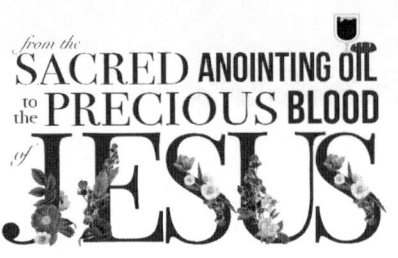

chapter 1

From the Sacred Anointing Oil to the Precious Blood of Jesus

The entirety of the Bible constitutes a unified narrative centered upon the crucifixion of Jesus. The Old Testament narrates the story of "To the cross," while the Four Gospels recount the story of "The cross" of Jesus Christ, the Son of God, the Lamb of God, who perfected the kingdom of God with a single sacrifice in the heavenly sanctuary. The writings from Acts to the Epistles, on the other hand, narrate the story of "From the cross." Consequently, an examination of the 66 books of the Bible in their entirety will reveal that the Bible is, in essence, the story of the cross of Jesus Christ and the narrative of God's love.

It is incumbent upon every Christian to study the Bible in a manner that is free from error, bias, and excessive interpretation. To achieve this, it is essential to identify the pivotal narratives that interconnect the various strands of the Bible and assess their significance. A comprehensive study of the Bible, from Genesis to Revelation, reveals the presence of pivotal narratives that serve to unify its disparate elements. To illustrate, the account of the "year-old lamb and the first Passover" in Exodus represents a pivotal narrative within the corpus of the Old Testament, particularly within the context of a kingdom of priests. Subsequently, in the New Testament, the "Lamb of God and the first Eucharist" in the four Gospels represents a pivotal narrative within the context of the kingdom of God.

What is the significance of the story of the year-old lamb and the first Passover in the book of Exodus within the context of the Old Testament? The first Passover in Egypt marked the inception of the priestly nation and its role as a "nation," as delineated by the five sacrifices. Subsequently, with the Passover lamb as a point of departure, God constituted the Levites, who were to succeed the firstborn of each family in Israel, as "public servants." These Levites were thus charged with the maintenance of the priestly system. In the absence of a nation, the concept of an office is rendered meaningless.

In this way, the office of a kingdom of priests was inaugurated at the first Passover, and the kingdom of God, which would be perfected 1,500 years later when the Lamb of God, Jesus Christ, said on the cross, "It is finished," and the office of the Christian who would carry on that kingdom, was foreshadowed at the first Communion. When considered collectively, these two narratives can be seen to represent the "last Passover, first Eucharist." This unifies the Passover of a kingdom of priests, which lasted 1,500 years, and the Eucharist of the kingdom of God, which has spanned 2,000 years from the crucifixion of Jesus Christ. The term "tie" signifies an act of widening, deepening, or compressing.

The "first communion at the last Passover," which Jesus observed

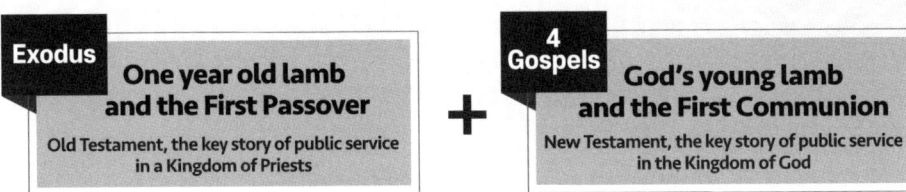

"Last Passover and First Communion"

Then Moses summoned all the elders of Israel and said to them,
Go at once and select the animals for your families and slaughter the Passover lamb (Exe 12:21)

The next day John saw Jesus coming toward him and said,
Look, the Lamb of God, who takes away the sin of the world! (Jn 1:29)

prior to his crucifixion, established the fundamental narrative that would persist until his second coming. Accordingly, Jesus desired to observe the first communion, thereby ensuring that it would serve to commemorate him, Jesus Christ, rather than merely the day of Passover.

The First Passover, celebrated for 1,500 Years

In the days preceding his crucifixion, Jesus was aware that this would be his final Passover. He informed his disciples, with whom he had shared a symbiotic relationship for three years, that he wished to and required for his spiritual sustenance to partake in the Passover ritual.

"I have eagerly desired to partake in this Passover meal with you." In emphasizing his desire to partake in the Passover meal with his disciples, Jesus underscores the significance of this ritual for him.

"And he said to them,
"I have eagerly desired to eat this Passover with you before I suffer.
For I tell you, I will not eat it again until it finds fulfillment
in the kingdom of God." (Luke 22:15-16)

Jesus had been awaiting this occasion for a considerable length of time, ever since he had summoned his disciples to the shores of Galilee three years prior. Moreover, this anticipation extended even further back to the "first Passover" in Egypt, which had occurred 1,500 years earlier.

One might posit that the "first Passover," which occurred 1,500 years ago, can be considered a "shadow of the first Eucharist." The first Passover was an imperative directive from God at the conclusion of Moses' ninth exodus dialogue with Pharaoh, the king of Egypt. Following the collapse of negotiations between Pharaoh and Moses, the Hebrew people were understandably fearful for their future in Egypt. The prospect of continued hardship and suffering, coupled with the lack of hope for an imminent exodus, must have been overwhelming. However, God was preparing the most significant miracle of all: through Moses, God designated a day and instructed each family in Israel to slay a "lamb."

The Hebrew people were enslaved in Egypt, compelled to labor as bricklayers and farmers for the Egyptians. It is noteworthy that they did not succumb to panic in response to God's abrupt directive to slay a "lamb." On the night in question, approximately 23,000 families complied with the divine directive by slaying a year-old lamb, immersing it in fresh hyssop, and affixing it to the doorposts and lintels of their dwellings. They then roasted the carcass over an open fire, consuming it with unleavened bread and bitter herbs. This was done while wearing loincloths around their waists, shoes on their feet, and staffs in their hands.

In the event that the directive to apply the blood of a one-year-old lamb to the doorposts and lintels of each residence was not adhered to, the firstborn of the Egyptians, the firstborn of the Hebrews, and the firstborn of any animal would perish. The reason for the Hebrew people's ability to procure a sufficient number of one-year-old lambs for every household in a single effort, despite their enslavement in Egypt, can be traced back to the narratives of their ancestors, Joseph and Jacob.

Jacob, son of Isaac, fled to Harran to avoid conflict with his brother Esau. Following a period of several years in Harran, Jacob demonstrated remarkable proficiency in shepherding and amassed a considerable flock of sheep. This included the innovative practice of using the barked branches of a cypress tree to shear the lambs, as recorded in Genesis 30:37-43. It is evident that this was only made possible by divine intervention (Genesis 31:8-12). Jacob proceeded to lead his newly acquired flocks through Canaan and eventually into Egypt. Joseph built on Jacob's pastoralist foundation by gathering the 70 or so families he had brought into the land of Goshen. He engaged them in pastoralism, which was an abomination to the Egyptians, in order to preserve the lineage and make them a great nation. Subsequently, 430 years later, prior to the Exodus, the Hebrew people were enslaved in Egypt. However, through pastoralism, each family was prepared to celebrate the first Passover by slaughtering a year-old lamb.

The first Passover in Egypt was a pivotal moment in history, marking the survival of the Hebrew people's firstborn and the establishment of a kingdom of priests. In contrast, the death of all the firstborn in Egypt resulted in the destruction of the entire foundation of the nation's

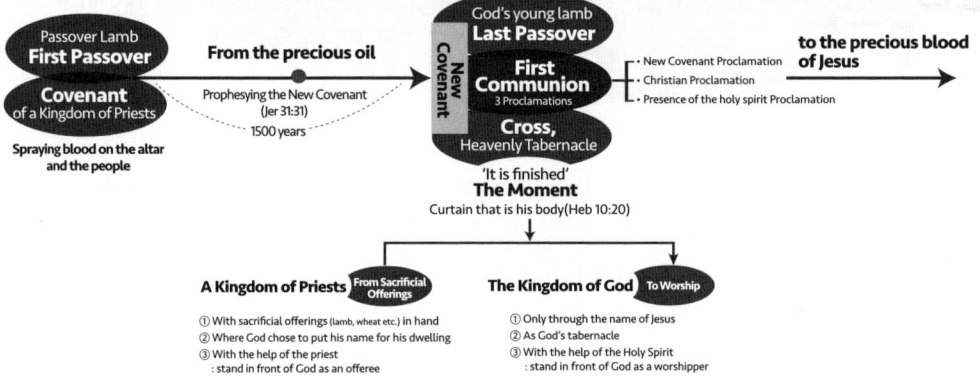

The days are coming, declares the Lord, when I will make a new covenant with the people of Israel and with the people of Judah (Jer 31:31)

by a new and living way opened for us through the curtain, that is, his body (Heb 10:20)

The Signs on the Door | James Tissot 作

empire. For the Hebrew people, or Israel, the first Passover became a significant marker in the establishment of a kingdom of priests. Over 1,500 years later, Jesus is introduced by John the Baptist as the "Lamb of God who takes away the sin of the world." John the Baptist's reference to the "Lamb of God" is based on the "Passover lamb."

"The blood will be a sign for you on the houses where you are,
and when I see the blood, I will pass over you.
No destructive plague will touch you when I strike Egypt.
This is a day you are to commemorate;
for the generations to come you shall celebrate
it as a festival to the Lord—a lasting ordinance." (Exodus 12:13-14)

The reason Passover was able to continue for over 1,500 years while the kingdom of priests remained is because, at the time of its institution, God commanded that it be celebrated as a feast to the LORD, to be observed from generation to generation as an everlasting ordinance.

The Israelites, who had entered into a holy civil covenant with God as a kingdom of priests, celebrated the first Passover in Egypt and the second at Mount Sinai after the Exodus. While the initial Passover was observed as a matter of obedience, with the participants lacking a comprehensive understanding of its significance, the subsequent Passover was a joyous occasion, marked by the Israelites' gratitude for divine benevolence and contemplation on the day's import as they emerged from bondage and attained liberation (Num. 9:5). This is why the second Passover in the wilderness marked the inception of a celebration that was to be observed from generation to generation as an eternal observance.

After 40 years in the wilderness, the Israelites have finally ceased their reliance on manna from heaven as their primary source of sustenance. They crossed the Jordan River into Canaan, the Promised Land, with aspirations of becoming the Manna Generation and commemorating Passover. However, before they could fully conquer the land, the Manna Generation celebrated Passover on the plains of Jericho. At this juncture, the Passover celebration marks the conclusion of the 40-year period during which God provided manna as a sustenance.

"On the evening of the fourteenth day of the month,
while camped at Gilgal on the plains of Jericho,
the Israelites celebrated the Passover. The day after the Passover,
that very day, they ate some of the produce of the land:
unleavened bread and roasted grain.
The manna stopped the day after they ate this food from the land;
there was no longer any manna for the Israelites,
but that year they ate the produce of Canaan." (Joshua 5:10-12)

The Israelites, descendants of Abraham, entered the promised land of Canaan and were allotted a portion of the land. However, during the 350-year period of the Judges, they maintained a kingdom of priests but did not observe the holidays and festivals, including Passover. Instead, they were subjected to the plagues and disgorgements outlined in the Book of Leviticus. Subsequently, Samuel reestablished a kingdom of priests and observed Passover in accordance with the priestly laws. Additionally, David had a vision of constructing a temple to house the ark of God's covenant. God expressed satisfaction with David's vision and, through the prophet Nathan, provided him with the architectural plans for the Jerusalem temple. He also promised to bless David's son, ensuring that he would oversee its construction. In essence, God conveyed that David's dynasty and kingdom would be safeguarded, and that his lineage would enjoy enduring stability and authority. The temple was constructed under the direction of Solomon, David's son, and Jerusalem became the focal point of a kingdom of priests, where Passover, the Feasts of the Seven Days, and the Feast of Tabernacles were observed (2 Chron. 8:12-13).

"Then to the place the Lord your God will choose as a dwelling for his Name—there you are to bring everything I command you: your burnt offerings and sacrifices, your tithes and special gifts, and all the choice possessions you have vowed to the Lord."
(Deuteronomy 12:11)

All the people of Israel, who had entered into a covenant with God according to the laws God had given them, came to the temple in Jerusalem every year to celebrate Passover, "the day of the Lord," and to sacrifice to God. Subsequently, following Solomon's demise and the partition of Israel into two kingdoms, one situated to the north and the other to the south, God bestowed the authority of the ten tribes of northern Israel upon Jeroboam, stipulating that he safeguard Jerusalem, the city God had anointed as a sacred site, as a prerequisite. Despite the nation's division, the directive was for the people of the ten tribes to descend to Jerusalem for the celebration of Passover at the Temple in Jerusalem.

"I will take the kingdom from his son's hands and give you ten tribes.
I will give one tribe to his son so that David my servant may always have a lamp before me in Jerusalem,
the city where I chose to put my Name.
However, as for you, I will take you,
and you will rule over all that your heart desires;
you will be king over Israel.
If you do whatever I command you and walk in obedience to me and do what is right in my eyes by obeying my decrees and commands,
as David my servant did, I will be with you.
I will build you a dynasty as enduring as the one I built for David and will give Israel to you." (1 Kings 11:35-38)

However, Jeroboam contravened the divine edicts and exploited the priestly population for his own ends. He altered the holidays and feasts of a kingdom of priests, including Passover, designated non-Levites as priests, and relocated the place of worship by constructing the golden calf at Dan and Bethel instead of Jerusalem. This effectively prevented the people of northern Israel from attending the temple in Jerusalem three times a year.

"If these people go up to offer sacrifices at the temple of the Lord in Jerusalem, they will again give their allegiance to their lord, Rehoboam king of Judah.
They will kill me and return to King Rehoboam.
After seeking advice, the king made two golden calves.
He said to the people, It is too much for you to go up to Jerusalem.
Here are your gods, Israel, who brought you up out of Egypt.

One he set up in Bethel, and the other in Dan." (1 Kings 12:27-29)

Northern Israel subsequently embraced the tenets of Jeroboam for two centuries, ultimately becoming a racially mixed community of Samaritans. This occurred as Northern Israel was subjugated by the Assyrian Empire, which was regarded as the instrument of divine retribution. For a period of eight centuries, they were subjected to ostracism and repudiation before being restored by Jesus.

As Hezekiah, king of southern Judah, observed the devastation of northern Israel, he came to understand that God's intention was to maintain the integrity of a kingdom of priests, even if it entailed the division of Israel into two distinct entities. Hezekiah dispatched emissaries to all of Israel, from Dan to Beersheba, and to the ten tribes of northern Israel, extending an invitation to them to join him in Jerusalem to observe the Passover. Hezekiah extended an invitation to the northern Israelites to convene in Jerusalem, citing the city's sacred significance as the chosen location for the divine name of the Lord to be enshrined within the temple. Moreover, it was in Jerusalem that the entire nation would collectively observe the Passover ritual, marking the inception of a kingdom of priests. However, upon hearing Hezekiah's appeal, the northern Israelites responded with derision and ridicule. Nevertheless, a fortunate number of northern Israelites, albeit a small one, humbled themselves and came down to Jerusalem.

"They decided to send a proclamation throughout Israel,
from Beersheba to Dan, calling the people to come to Jerusalem and celebrate the Passover to the Lord, the God of Israel.

It had not been celebrated in large numbers according to what was written. At the king's command,
couriers went throughout Israel and Judah with letters from the king and from his officials, which read:
People of Israel, return to the Lord, the God of Abraham, Isaac and Israel, that he may return to you who are left, who have escaped from the hand of the kings of Assyria." (2 Chronicles 30:5-6)

Hezekiah was unable to celebrate the Passover according to the written regulations for two reasons. Firstly, there was a shortage of sanctified priests. Secondly, the people were unable to gather in Jerusalem by the appointed time. Consequently, Hezekiah was compelled to postpone the Passover by a month, in accordance with the directives outlined in the Book of Numbers (Numbers 9:10-12). Subsequently, the populace of northern Israel and southern Judah, along with the resident and visiting foreigners, assembled in Jerusalem to observe the long-absent Passover, and they all expressed joy (2 Chronicles 30:21).

"They slaughtered the Passover lamb on the fourteenth day of the second month.
The priests and the Levites were ashamed and consecrated themselves and brought burnt offerings to the temple of the Lord.
Then they took up their regular positions as prescribed in the Law of Moses the man of God.
The priests splashed against the altar the blood handed to them by the Levites." (2 Chronicles 30:15-16)

Subsequently, King Josiah of Judah initiated a significant reform movement, with the observance of Passover as a pivotal element. This marked the first occasion since the time of Samuel that Passover was duly observed in accordance with the original Mosaic prescriptions.

"Josiah celebrated the Passover to the Lord in Jerusalem, and the Passover lamb was slaughtered on the fourteenth day of the first month. He appointed the priests to their duties and encouraged them in the service of the Lord's temple. He said to the Levites, who instructed all Israel and who had been consecrated to the Lord: "Put the sacred ark in the temple that Solomon son of David king of Israel built. It is not to be carried about on your shoulders. Now serve the Lord your God and his people Israel. Prepare yourselves by families in your divisions, according to the instructions written by David king of Israel and by his son Solomon.
"Stand in the holy place with a group of Levites for each subdivision of the families of your fellow Israelites, the lay people. Slaughter the Passover lambs, consecrate yourselves and prepare the lambs for your fellow Israelites, doing what the Lord commanded through Moses."
Josiah provided for all the lay people who were there a total of thirty thousand lambs and goats for the Passover offerings, and also three thousand cattle—all from the king's own possessions.
His officials also contributed voluntarily to the people and the priests and Levites. Hilkiah, Zechariah and Jehiel, the officials in charge of God's temple, gave the priests twenty-six hundred Passover offerings and three hundred cattle. Also Konaniah along with Shemaiah and Nethanel, his brothers, and Hashabiah, Jeiel and Jozabad, the leaders of the Levites, provided five thousand Passover offerings and five hundred head of cattle for the Levites.

The service was arranged and the priests stood in their places with the Levites in their divisions as the king had ordered. The Passover lambs were slaughtered, and the priests splashed against the altar the blood handed to them, while the Levites skinned the animals. They set aside the burnt offerings to give them to the subdivisions of the families of the people to offer to the Lord, as it is written in the Book of Moses. They did the same with the cattle. They roasted the Passover animals over the fire as prescribed, and boiled the holy offerings in pots, caldrons and pans and served them quickly to all the people. After this, they made preparations for themselves and for the priests, because the priests, the descendants of Aaron, were sacrificing the burnt offerings and the fat portions until nightfall. So the Levites made preparations for themselves and for the Aaronic priests.

The musicians, the descendants of Asaph, were in the places prescribed by David, Asaph, Heman and Jeduthun the king's seer. The gatekeepers at each gate did not need to leave their posts, because their fellow Levites made the preparations for them.

So at that time the entire service of the Lord was carried out for the celebration of the Passover and the offering of burnt offerings on the altar of the Lord, as King Josiah had ordered. The Israelites who were present celebrated the Passover at that time and observed the Festival of Unleavened Bread for seven days. The Passover had not been observed like this in Israel since the days of the prophet Samuel; and none of the kings of Israel had ever celebrated such a Passover as did Josiah, with the priests, the Levites and all Judah and Israel who were there with the people of Jerusalem. This Passover was celebrated in the eighteenth year of Josiah's reign." (2 Chronicles 35:1-19)

At the conclusion of the 500-year reign and following 70 years of Babylonian captivity, the Jews returned to Jerusalem. During this period, a kingdom of priests underwent a significant transformation, becoming a highly sought-after commodity. Through the efforts of Nehemiah and Ezra, a kingdom of priests restored a range of traditions, including sacrifices, feasts, and holidays. This restoration coincided with the Persian Empire's investment policy in the Levant.

"On the fourteenth day of the first month,
the exiles celebrated the Passover.
The priests and Levites had purified themselves
and were all ceremonially clean.
The Levites slaughtered the Passover lamb for all the exiles,
for their relatives the priests and for themselves." (Ezra 6:19-20)

The observation of this 'day' of Passover represented the most significant event in the Jewish nation's religious calendar for 1,500 years. The observance of Passover continued until the time of Jesus. The Gospel of Luke records that when Jesus was twelve years old, he accompanied his parents to the temple for the Passover holiday, in accordance with the laws governing the priestly nation.

"Every year Jesus' parents went to Jerusalem
for the Festival of the Passover.
When he was twelve years old, they went up to the festival,
according to the custom." (Luke 2:41-42)

Following the rule of Nehemiah and Ezra, Judea experienced the influence of the Hellenistic and Roman empires. It remained centered on the Jerusalem Temple until the advent of Jesus. Consequently, the Roman Empire governed Judea as a colony while maintaining a policy of deference towards the Jerusalem Temple. One of the methods by which the Roman Empire demonstrated respect for Passover as a Jewish holiday was through the implementation of a 'Passover Amnesty.' This ensured the continued functionality of the Temple and its associated rituals, which is why Jesus celebrated Passover annually. Ultimately, Jesus was able to commence the 'work of God' that he had been anticipating for an extended period. This is the inaugural 'communion' at the final Passover.

 2

The Passover lamb, offerings, and public servant

The term 'lamb' is, first and foremost, a sacrificial narrative. The burnt lamb offered by Abraham and Isaac, the Passover lamb provided by Moses, the sin offering presented by the high priest, the sacrificial lamb of John the Baptist, the Lamb of God, and the Lamb of Revelation. Secondly, the term 'Lamb' represents the narrative of the mission of the high priestly 'office' of a kingdom of priests, which subsequently leads to the mission of the high priestly 'office' of Jesus, the kingly high priest of the kingdom of God. This, in turn, leads to the story of the once-for-all sacrifice of the cross, which represents the righteousness of God. This is the mission of the 'anointed one.'

The narrative of the 'lamb' story commences with Abraham's burnt offering on Mount Moriah.

On their way to Mount Moriah to sacrifice to God, Isaac poses a question to his father Abraham.

"Isaac spoke up and said to his father Abraham,
"Father?"
"Yes, my son?" Abraham replied.
"The fire and wood are here," Isaac said,
"but where is the lamb for the burnt offering?" Abraham answered,
"God himself will provide the lamb for the burnt offering, my son."
… Abraham looked up and there in a thicket he saw a ram caught by its horns.
He went over and took the ram and sacrificed it as a burnt offering instead of his son." (Genesis 22:7-13)

In response to Isaac's inquiry regarding the lamb for the burnt offering, Abraham asserted that God would provide for himself, a concept known as "Jehovah-Jireh," and indeed, God did provide a ram. God's provision enabled Abraham to take the ram and offer the burnt offering "on behalf" of his son Isaac.

Over five centuries later, in Egypt, the "first Passover lamb" saved all the firstborn of Israel.

"On that same night I will pass through Egypt and strike down every firstborn of both people and animals,
and I will bring judgment on all the gods of Egypt.
I am the Lord. The blood will be a sign for you on the houses where you are, and when I see the blood, I will pass over you.
No destructive plague will touch you when I strike Egypt.

Abraham and Isaac | Gainsborough Dupont 作

Jesus and the Passover

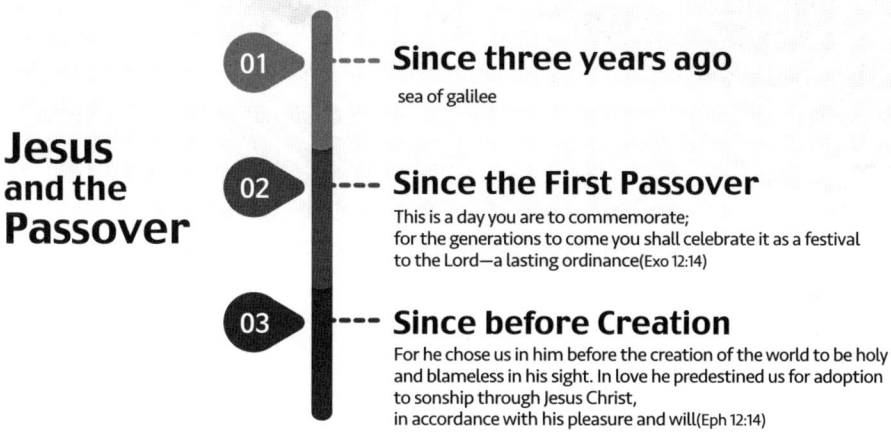

01 ---- **Since three years ago**
sea of galilee

02 ---- **Since the First Passover**
This is a day you are to commemorate;
for the generations to come you shall celebrate it as a festival
to the Lord—a lasting ordinance(Exo 12:14)

03 ---- **Since before Creation**
For he chose us in him before the creation of the world to be holy
and blameless in his sight. In love he predestined us for adoption
to sonship through Jesus Christ,
in accordance with his pleasure and will(Eph 12:14)

For he chose us in him before the creation of the world to be holy and blameless in his sight.
In love he predestined us for adoption to sonship through Jesus Christ,
in accordance with his pleasure and will (Eph 1:4-5)

"This is a day you are to commemorate; for the generations to come you shall celebrate it as a festival to the Lord—a lasting ordinance." (Exodus 12:12-14)

In essence, this is the Egyptian judgment. Had the Hebrew people not obeyed God's command, they would have suffered the same judgment as Egypt. However, on that night, they obeyed God's command. They selected a lamb for the Passover sacrifice, designated by the number of their families, and applied its blood to the doorposts and lintel on the right and left with hyssop. They roasted the meat over a fire and ate it with unleavened bread and bitter herbs. As a consequence of their compliance on that occasion, the firstborn of the Hebrews and the firstborn of the animals survived, while Egypt perished. This included Pharaoh himself, along with all of the firstborn in his court, as well as the firstborn of the prisoners and the firstborn of the livestock. Subsequently, Pharaoh summoned Moses and Aaron and granted them permission to depart (Exodus 12:31-33). God intervened to spare the firstborn of Israel with the Passover lamb.

The nation established by the Sinai Covenant after the Exodus is a "kingdom of priests." The five sacrifices represent the core tenets of a kingdom of priests, including the burnt offering, sin offering, fellowship offering, guilt offering, and the sin offering. Sacrifice represents the conduit through which humans may engage with the divine and receive forgiveness. This is the sole avenue through which humans can engage with the divine.

"For the generations to come this burnt offering

is to be made regularly at the entrance to the tent of meeting,
before the Lord.
There I will meet you and speak to you;
there also I will meet with the Israelites,
and the place will be consecrated by my glory." (Exodus 29:42-43)

It is a fundamental tenet of ritual practice that an offering must be made. The quality of the offering must be of the highest standard. The priest was required to select the most valuable item from his possessions to present as an offering. This could be a lamb, a bull, two pigeons, or fine flour. Only when the offering was of the highest quality could the priest approach God and receive forgiveness for the sins of the people.

One might be well advised to consider the matter further. What could be offered to God, the creator of the entire universe, that would be an adequate expression of gratitude and reverence? One might inquire whether the offering of expensive jewelry would be pleasing to God. One might inquire whether God would be pleased with a house or a car as an offering. If we were invited to the residence of the wealthiest individual in the world, what gift would we present in order to demonstrate our appreciation and respect? Indeed, there is nothing that we can offer God. However, He has prescribed a sacrifice that we are to offer Him, and He has indicated that He will accept it if it is offered with sincerity and devotion. In order to express gratitude to God for facilitating forgiveness, all members of the Israelite community, who had entered into a covenant with the priestly class, were obliged to present sacrifices on a daily basis. Accordingly, the high priest, on behalf of the entire populace, presented sacrifices to God on a daily basis, at both the morning and evening hours, without fail. This is referred to as the "continual sacrifice".

"This is what you are to offer on the altar regularly each day:
two lambs a year old.
Offer one in the morning and the other at twilight.
With the first lamb offer a tenth of an ephah of the finest flour mixed with a quarter of a hin of oil from pressed olives,
and a quarter of a hin of wine as a drink offering.
Sacrifice the other lamb at twilight with the same grain offering and its drink offering as in the morning—a pleasing aroma, a food offering presented to the Lord.
"For the generations to come this burnt offering is to be made regularly at the entrance to the tent of meeting, before the Lord.
There I will meet you and speak to you." (Exodus 29:38-42)

In the daily morning and evening burnt offerings that the high priest makes, a year-old lamb serves as the principal offering, while the other three offerings (flour, oil, and wine) constitute the accompanying offerings. The latter refers to the pouring out of strong drink or wine over the sacrifice. It is incumbent upon the high priest to select the offerings with great care and present them to God. It is incumbent upon the high priest to select the most optimal offering. Firstly, it is incumbent upon the high priest to slaughter two lambs, one year old and unblemished, on a daily basis. Subsequently, the three offerings must be combined in accordance with the prescribed proportions, prepared meticulously, and the lambs must be burned once in the morning and once in the evening, before being presented to God. In the event of non-compliance with the prescribed ritual, the offender is subject to immediate death, as was the case with Nadab and Abihu. This is the high priest's continual offering.

The high priest repeated the weekly cycle on a daily basis for a period of 1,500 years in a nation where the priesthood was a dominant institution. While pointless repetition is inherently boring, necessary repetition is a fundamental aspect of any well-functioning system and serves the common good. The weekly repetition system, which has been in place since the dawn of human society, has remained largely unchanged despite the numerous transformations that have occurred in human society.

Over the course of 1,500 years, numerous sacrifices were made to God. If one were to include the High Priest's burnt offerings and Passover, the total number of sacrifices would exceed one million. This signifies that a lamb, approximately one year of age, was presented to God on over a million occasions. This is the origin of the Lamb of God. Consequently, over the course of 1,500 years, the procedures associated with the sacrifices had been sufficiently mastered and practiced. This enabled John the Baptist, upon seeing Jesus, to declare, "Behold, the Lamb of God who takes away the sin of the world" (John 1:29), and for this assertion to be immediately comprehended by all. The repeated sacrifices thus paved the way for the emergence of the once-for-all sacrifice of Jesus, the Lamb of God. It is remarkable that the once-for-all sacrifice of Jesus emerged in history after so many meaningful repetitions. The sacrifice of Jesus on the cross represents the pinnacle of divine righteousness.

In this way, Jesus became the "Lamb of God" and the sacrifice for humanity. It is difficult to envisage how the narrative of "eat my flesh and drink my blood" could have emerged without the premise of the sacrifice of the Lamb of God. The narrative of the Old Testament is pervaded by the motif of the flesh and blood of Jesus. A thorough reading of the Old Testament reveals that every narrative is a divinely orchestrated account, ultimately culminating in the revelation of Jesus Christ. The concept of grace is best exemplified by the sacrificial act of Jesus Christ, who became a ransom for our salvation. This supreme act of grace allows us to live when we believe in Jesus, the Lamb of God, as our redeeming Savior. The word "lamb" is etymologically derived from the term "shed blood." The blood that Jesus shed as the Lamb of God on the cross was blood that was shed as a ransom.

"Just as the Son of Man did not come to be served, but to serve,
and to give his life as a ransom for many." (Matthew 20:28)

The Apostle Paul was keenly aware of the connection between the Passover lamb and Jesus.

"For just as through the disobedience of the one man the many were made sinners, so also through the obedience of the one man the many will be made righteous." (Romans 5:19)

"Get rid of the old yeast,
so that you may be a new unleavened batch—as you really are.

For Christ, our Passover lamb, has been sacrificed." (1 Corinthians 5:7)

Additionally, in the Book of Revelation, Jesus is referred to as "Lamb" on 28 occasions, more frequently than he is referred to as "Jesus" on 12 occasions. The name "Lamb" is written more frequently than the name "Jesus" in reference to the throne of God.

"And they cried out in a loud voice:
"Salvation belongs to our God,
who sits on the throne,
and to the Lamb." (Revelation 7:10)

One might inquire as to why the Book of Revelation employs this term with such frequency. This is because the term "lamb" fully acknowledges the grace of Jesus' singular sacrifice on the cross.

From Exodus to Revelation, one of the principal themes that runs throughout the Bible is that of the Lamb. Prior to the crucifixion of Jesus, the Lamb of God served as the focal point, represented by a year-old lamb. From the moment of the crucifixion to the first Eucharist, the Lamb of God remained at the center of the narrative. This concrete narrative is what animates our hearts.

Secondly, the Passover lamb leads to public servants in a kingdom of priests.

In the inaugural Passover in Egypt, God designated the firstborn of each family whose lives were spared as His own. Following a census, the Levites were selected as a replacement group for the firstborn of the twelve tribes, claimed as God's own, and established as a kingdom of priests.

"Every firstborn male in Israel, whether human or animal, is mine.
When I struck down all the firstborn in Egypt,
I set them apart for myself.
And I have taken the Levites in place of all the firstborn sons in Israel."
(Numbers 8:17-18)

In other words, God established a system of twelve plus one, resulting in a total of thirteen tribes. God divided the Israelites into the twelve tribes, who were allotted land in Canaan and were expected to live off the land and pay tithes, and the tribe of Levi, who were not allotted land and were to serve as priestly officials. The Levites are the descendants of Levi's sons, Gershon, Kohath, and Merari. The Levites were distinguished from other Israelites by their gender, age, and social status. They were male, over one month old, and between the ages of 30 and 50. Normally, men of the twelve tribes would have been set apart as adults at age 20 to pursue a profession and engage in battle. However, the Levites underwent an additional ten years of preparation to serve in the temple at age 20, subsequently retiring from active duty at age 50. Following their retirement from active duty, it is likely that they assumed responsibility for the education of Levites aged 30 and below. This is due to the fact that the Levites were established as the "consecrated" or "public servants" in a kingdom of priests.

In particular, God, through Moses, anointed the heads of Aaron, a member of the tribe of Levi, and his sons, thereby establishing the family of Aaron as the high priests.

"Anoint them just as you anointed their father,
so they may serve me as priests.
Their anointing will be to a priesthood that will continue throughout their generations." (Exodus 40:15)

The oil used for anointing the priest's head was a "sacred anointing oil," the preparation of which was taught by God Himself. The pouring and application of the anointing oil constituted a pivotal aspect of the establishment of the priestly office. The question thus arises as to the method of preparation of the anointing oil.

"Take the following fine spices: 500 shekels of liquid myrrh, half as much (that is, 250 shekels) of fragrant cinnamon, 250 shekels of fragrant calamus, 500 shekels of cassia—all according to the sanctuary shekel—and a hi of olive oil.
Make these into a sacred anointing oil, a fragrant blend, the work of a perfumer. It will be the sacred anointing oil.
Then use it to anoint the tent of meeting, the ark of the covenant law, the table and all its articles, the lampstand and its accessories, the altar of incense, the altar of burnt offering and all its utensils, and the basin with its stand. You shall consecrate them so they will be most holy, and whatever touches them will be holy.
"Anoint Aaron and his sons and consecrate them so they may serve me as priests. Say to the Israelites, 'This is to be my sacred anointing oil for the generations to come.

El sumo sacerdote Aarón | Juan de Juanes 作

· Sacred anointing oil

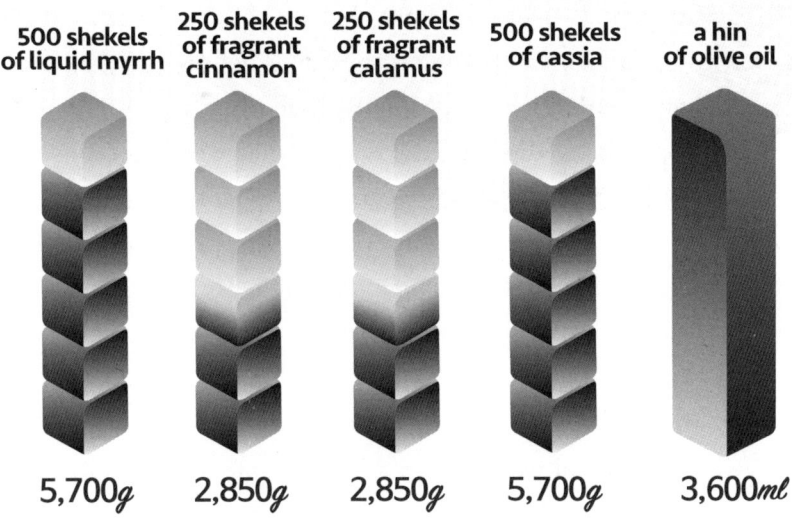

Anoint Aaron and his sons and consecrate them so they may serve me as priests.
Say to the Israelites, This is to be my sacred anointing oil for the generations to come (Exo 30:30-31)

Do not pour it on anyone else's body and do not make any other oil using the same formula. It is sacred, and you are to consider it sacred. Whoever makes perfume like it and puts it on anyone other than a priest must be cut off from their people.'" (Exodus 30:23-33)

The anointing oil is composed of five principal ingredients. The recipe calls for 500 shekels of myrrh, 250 shekels of broilers, 250 shekels of irises, 500 shekels of cinnamon, and one heaping tablespoon of olive oil. Upon combining the aforementioned five ingredients in the specified proportions, the result is a substance designated as "holy oil." This recipe was not transmitted through folklore; it was explicitly conveyed by divine revelation. In creating the proportions for the production of the holy oil, God, who made the heavens and the earth in harmony, focused on harmonizing the 1,500 years of His rule.

The question thus arises as to the manner in which the "holy oil" was employed. The holy oil was used to anoint or sprinkle the holy objects of the sanctuary, with the purpose of setting them apart as holy. This included all the utensils of the sanctuary, such as the tabernacle, the ark of the testimony, the statues, the lampstand, the altar of incense, the altar of burnt offering, the waterpot, and the laver. Despite the fact that Bezalel and Oholiab crafted the items designated for the sanctuary in accordance with the specifications outlined in the divine plan, they did not attain the status of holiness until the completion of the fabrication process. It was only upon anointing the utensils with the requisite anointing oil, as God had commanded, that they became holy. The instruments were sanctified and set apart in the sanctuary, to be touched and viewed only in accordance with the laws of a kingdom of priests.

Furthermore, God anointed Aaron and his sons with oil, thereby sanctifying them. The anointing oil was not intended for general application; rather, it was reserved for priests, as prescribed by the laws of a kingdom of priests. Accordingly, God commanded that the anointing oil not be manufactured. In the event of commercial production, both the manufacturer and the individual receiving the anointing were to be put to death. God commanded that the anointing oil be made in accordance with the proportions provided and used exclusively by priests on holy objects.

In a ceremony conducted by Moses, Aaron and his sons were anointed and commissioned as priests, thereby establishing them as officials within a kingdom of priests. It is essential that a nation maintain an appropriate ratio of officials to its population, or, in other words, an appropriate ratio of priests to people. To illustrate, at the inaugural Passover in Egypt, the Hebrews' cohort of firstborn and the number of yearling lambs they sacrificed by family unit enumeration demonstrated an unquestionable ratio. This is why God established the tribe of Levi in place of the firstborn to administer the priestly system (Numbers 3:44-51). This constituted the optimal ratio of officers for maintaining a kingdom of priests.

However, it was not a straightforward process for Aaron's family, belonging to the tribe of Levi, to become the high priest, an official within a kingdom of priests. Aaron's two sons, Nadab and Abihu, were killed for offering the incorrect sacrifice, which serves as a cautionary tale for the priesthood (Leviticus 10:1-7).

Following the incident at Kadesh-Barnea, the rebellion of Korah, Dathan, and Abiram against their leader Moses and their refusal to acknowledge Aaron as high priest resulted in a plague that swept through the people. At this juncture, Moses petitioned for divine pardon by having Aaron bear the censer and traverse the populace in the vicinity of the afflicted area (Num. 16:46-48). In light of these circumstances, the priesthood was a matter of life and death. God even granted Aaron's staff a miracle of blossoming and fruitfulness, thereby establishing the priestly authority of a kingdom of priests (Num. 17:1-8).

Subsequently, the anointing, which symbolizes the appointment to public office in a nation of priests, is transferred from the high priest to the "king." Saul, the first king of Israel, was anointed, yet this anointing could not be transferred to his son, Jonathan, as Saul had intended. This is because Saul exercised undue influence by concentrating power in his own tribe, the tribe of Benjamin, rather than pursuing a more inclusive approach that would have reflected the values of a nation of priests. The nation's governance is the responsibility of God. Subsequently, David was anointed king by the twelve tribes and ascended to the throne. However, there was no guarantee that his descendants would necessarily continue to reign. However, when David recounted his dream of "building the temple" to Nathan, God spoke to him through Nathan, imparting a significant message.

"When your days are over and you rest with your ancestors,
I will raise up your offspring to succeed you,

your own flesh and blood, and I will establish his kingdom.
He is the one who will build a house for my Name,
and I will establish the throne of his kingdom forever." (2 Samuel 7:12-13)

God's promise to "establish your throne forever" is conveyed to David's son Solomon, who is anointed king.

"Zadok the priest took the horn of oil from the sacred tent
and anointed Solomon.
Then they sounded the trumpet and all the people shouted,
"Long live King Solomon!" (1 Kings 1:39)

The anointing of priestly national office was expanded from "high priest" to "king" through the actions of Elijah, who also established the role of prophet. In response to the failure of northern Israel to fulfill its priestly duties, God, through the prophet Elijah, withheld rain for several years. Following a three-year drought, Elijah confronted King Ahab and proceeded to kill 450 prophets of Baal on Mount Carmel. However, Queen Jezebel remained undaunted and vowed to kill Elijah. Therefore, Elijah was compelled to flee, despite his triumph at Mount Carmel. Upon reaching Mount Horeb, Elijah made two appeals to God, using the same words on each occasion.

"He replied, "I have been very zealous for the Lord God Almighty.
The Israelites have rejected your covenant,
torn down your altars, and put your prophets to death with the sword.
I am the only one left, and now they are trying to kill me too."
(1 Kings 19:10,14)

Subsequently, God bestowed upon Elijah a significant mission.

"The Lord said to him,
"Go back the way you came, and go to the Desert of Damascus.
When you get there, anoint Hazael king over Aram.
Also, anoint Jehu son of Nimshi king over Israel,
and anoint Elisha son of Shaphat
from Abel Meholah to succeed you as prophet." (1 Kings 19:15-16)

In addition to anointing Elisha through Elijah, God also anointed "prophets," thereby conferring upon them the responsibilities and duties associated with the priestly office.

The initial Passover "lamb" subsequently acquired the connotations of "sacrifice" and "anointing, office." As the anointing continued for 1,500 years in a kingdom of priests, it gave rise to the "messianic idea" and ultimately led to the advent of Jesus Christ. In the Christian tradition, Jesus Christ is regarded as an anointed, kingly high priest, prophet, and the Lamb of God who became a sacrifice. According to this tradition, Jesus entered the heavenly sanctuary not made with hands and atoned for our sins through a single sacrifice. Jesus' sacrifice was a singular event, yet it was accomplished through the shedding of his blood on the cross. This blood is referred to as the "Precious Blood of Jesus." Ultimately, in the Book of Revelation, the Lamb, Jesus Christ, is depicted as occupying the throne of God, symbolizing his status as the "one who has overcome." This imagery serves to reinforce the promise of being seated alongside him in that exalted position.

"To the one who is victorious,
I will give the right to sit with me on my throne,
just as I was victorious and sat down with my Father on his throne."
(Revelation 3:21)

 3

Anointing Oil and Blood:
A Path to Forgiveness of Sins

From a theological perspective, humans are sinners before the righteous God. The consequence of sin is death. However, God desires to forgive and save humanity from the consequences of sin, and thus devised a plan of salvation. One such plan is the first Passover in Egypt, in which the Egyptian firstborn were unable to obtain forgiveness for their sins. However, in contrast to the fate of the Egyptian firstborn, the Hebrew firstborn were able to survive and avoid death. The question thus arises as to why.

The Hebrew people were instructed by God to follow a specific method for the forgiveness of sins, and they did so. The method by which the Hebrew people were granted forgiveness and granted life was through the shedding of the blood of a one-year-old lamb. The application of the blood of the one-year-old lamb to the doorposts and seals on the right and left was a demonstration of obedience, and it was through this act that the firstborn of each family in the Hebrew nation was forgiven. Nevertheless, the sacrifice of the one-year-old lamb in Egypt and its association with the firstborn was a singular occurrence. The nation that emerged subsequently was founded upon this event and became a nation of priests.

"Speak to the Israelites and say to them:
'When anyone among you brings an offering to the Lord,
bring as your offering an animal from either the herd or the flock."
(Leviticus 1:2)

"In this way the priest will make atonement for them before the Lord, and they will be forgiven for any of the things they did that made them guilty." (Leviticus 6:7)

The assertion that "whosoever ⋯ shall have forgiveness of sins" represents an extraordinary proclamation by the divine entity. In the Book of Leviticus, God has established a system of atonement for all individuals, regardless of their transgressions. This system comprises five types of sacrifices, which can be offered in three distinct ways: burnt offerings, sin offerings, fellowship offerings, guilt offerings, and sin offerings. The decision of how to prepare the offering is at the discretion of the individual. It is simply a matter of preparing the offering meticulously and bringing it with you. Nevertheless, it is of greater consequence that the offering be presented with the assistance of a priest in a location designated for the invocation of Jehovah's name. Accordingly, the necessity for an official to oversee the sacrificial process emerges, which is where the term "priest" becomes pertinent.

The priests who officiate at the sacrifices are individuals who have experienced forgiveness themselves. In selecting the Levites to represent the firstborn, God demonstrated His willingness to bestow forgiveness upon those who had demonstrated obedience at the inaugural Passover. Furthermore, He appointed Aaron as high priest, entrusting him with the responsibilities of a priestly office and pouring the "anointing oil" that He had previously commanded Moses to make. The term "anointing oil" was subsequently applied to kings and prophets, in addition to the officials of a kingdom of priests.

The subsequent crucial stipulation pertains to the designation of the sacrificial site. This was to be situated in a location designated as the place where Jehovah's name would be invoked, and in close proximity to the Ark of the Covenant, which housed the stone tablets inscribed with the Ten Commandments. Once constructed according to the prescribed blueprint and anointed, the Ark of the Covenant becomes a hallowed public space where the divine can be encountered in the act of sacrifice. The Tabernacle, with its Ark of the Covenant, thus constitutes the focal point where the priests, the public officials of a kingdom of priests, discharge their public duties.

This "atonement" was inextricably linked to the priest and the location of the sacrifice (the tabernacle, the temple). This was the only means by which forgiveness could be granted for any transgression. This system remained in place for 1,500 years. Subsequently, God established a single, unified system whereby the three requisite elements of the sacrifice could be fulfilled simultaneously and perpetually: the sacrifice itself, the priestly figure, and the designated location for the name of

- **Sacred anointing oil and the precious blood of Jesus**

Sacred anointing oil

① From the First Passover to the Covenant of Mt. Sinai ▶ New Covenant (First Communion)

Precious blood

② After Jesus' crucifixion ▶ All Christians to glorify God as the kingdom of priests

③ Prophesying the Pentecost at the First Communion

the Lord to be invoked. In other words, God provided His Son as the sacrifice, appointed His Son to fulfill the priestly office, and designated the cross as the site of this ultimate act of devotion. In this way, Christ, the anointed one, Jesus, atoned for the sins of a lifetime through a single sacrifice on the cross.

In Leviticus, the term "anyone" is understood to refer to the Israelites. In Jesus' singular sacrifice, the scope of "anyone" is "all nations." This is elucidated by Paul in Romans.

"This righteousness is given through faith
in Jesus Christ to all who believe.
There is no difference between Jew and Gentile." (Romans 3:22)

There is no discrimination among all nations for those who believe in Jesus Christ. This is an extraordinary testimony.

The righteousness of God toward those who believe in Jesus Christ—a righteousness attested to in both the Law and the Prophets—is "without distinction." In contrast to the kingdom of the priests, where those who offered sacrifices with the assistance of anointed priests were forgiven, the kingdom of God does not differentiate between those who receive forgiveness through faith in Jesus Christ. An extraordinary occurrence has transpired.

"And all are justified freely by his grace through the redemption that came by Christ Jesus.
God presented Christ as a sacrifice of atonement, through the shedding

of his blood—to be received by faith.
He did this to demonstrate his righteousness, because in his forbearance he had left the sins committed beforehand unpunished—" (Romans 3:24-25)

The term "sacrifice," or "the sacrifice that is in Jesus," encompasses the singular, definitive offering. In the absence of a sacrificial system within a kingdom of priests, the concept of a once-for-all sacrifice and propitiation would not exist. In providing the propitiation in Jesus Christ, God has made an invaluable contribution to the Christian faith.

"Now we know that whatever the law says,
it says to those who are under the law,
so that every mouth may be silenced
and the whole world held accountable to God." (Romans 3:19)

The advent of the law brought about a greater understanding of divine judgment.

"Therefore no one will be declared righteous in God's sight
by the works of the law;
rather, through the law we become conscious of our sin." (Romans 3:20)

The law serves to illustrate the extent of humanity's transgressions and underscores the necessity for forgiveness.

"But now apart from the law the righteousness of God
has been made known,
to which the Law and the Prophets testify." (Romans 3:21)

Last Passover the First Communion

From the sacred anointing oil to the precious blood of Jesus

sacred anointing oil → 1,500 years of regular burnt offerings → **3 Communion Proclamations** → The Once-for-all sacrifice on the cross → precious blood

A Kingdom of Priests

1. New Covenant Proclamation
2. Christian Proclamation
3. Presence of the holy spirit Proclamation

The Kingdom of God

Christ on the Cross | Bartolomé Esteban Murillo 作

The crucifixion of Jesus on Passover, the last Passover observed with his disciples after three years, his ascension to the role of high priest, and his crucifixion on a cross not made with hands in the heavenly sanctuary are all evidence of the law. In the absence of the law, these events could not have occurred. Furthermore, there is evidence provided by the prophets. To illustrate, the three days that Jonah spent in the belly of the fish allude to the three days that elapsed between Jesus' crucifixion and resurrection. In conclusion, the aforementioned evidence substantiates the assertion that these events are indicative of the law and the prophets.

"for all have sinned and fall short of the glory of God,
and all are justified freely by his grace through the redemption that came by Christ Jesus." (Romans 3:23-24)

As sinners, we are unable to perceive the glory of God. However, through Jesus Christ, we have been rendered righteous, not only receiving God's love and grace but also experiencing the revelation and imputation of God's righteousness, which enables us to glorify God.

"God presented Christ as a sacrifice of atonement,
through the shedding of his blood—to be received by faith.
He did this to demonstrate his righteousness,
because in his forbearance he had left the sins committed beforehand unpunished—" (Romans 3:25)

In establishing Jesus as a fellowship offering, God was articulating the necessity of Jesus and the significance of his blood. It was God who selected the one-year-old lamb for the inaugural Passover, and it was God who established the manner in which the sacrifice was to be prepared and presented within the context of a kingdom of priests. Ultimately, God determined that 1,500 years later, with the accumulated testimony of the law and the prophets, Jesus' blood would be the ultimate sacrifice. Jesus' obedience to God's will resulted in outcomes that are reflected in Romans 3:25. The overarching theme of Jesus' actions can be seen to be the significance of blood. However, Jesus did not conclude with this act of sacrifice; rather, he instructed his followers to continue commemorating his blood by partaking in the ritual of eating and drinking "the bread and wine."

The word "celebrate" encompasses the past, present, and future simultaneously. The entirety of past preparations collectively constitute the present, which in turn serves as a foundation for the future. In commemorating the "blood," it is our responsibility to fulfill the obligations of the Kingdom of God that Jesus entrusted to us. This responsibility is to disseminate the Christian joy that Paul discusses in Romans 3 to another individual. This is why Jesus designated his followers as "a kingdom and priests." The "joy of passing on" represents the fulfillment of the Great Commission. The act of consuming the body and blood of Jesus Christ signifies not merely an affirmation of belief and adherence to his teachings, but rather a transformation into a state of being that can be described as "people of Jesus," or, in other words, the establishment of a spiritual kingdom and the assumption of priestly roles. This is why the "blood" is of such significance.

The phrase "from the sacred oil to the blood" does not merely conclude with the resolution of the issue of sin and the bestowal of forgiveness; rather, it represents a strikingly jubilant mode of expression that encompasses both the obligation and the mission of attaining the status of a child who glorifies God and facilitating the ascension of another to that same status.

The commonality between anointing oil and blood is that they "flow," or communicate, and they impart life. The anointing oil served to establish public servants of a kingdom of priests whose role was to maintain the rule of God. This kingdom prepared for the arrival of the Messiah, Jesus Christ, who led a 1,500-year priestly nation through the use of anointing oil to establish the true kingdom of God. This entire narrative is recounted in David's Psalms.

The oil in question, which is of great value, ran down the beard of Aaron, even to his collar. This descent is likened to the dew that falls on the mountains of Zion.

"It is like precious oil poured on the head, running down on the beard, running down on Aaron's beard, down on the collar of his robe.
It is as if the dew of Hermon were falling on Mount Zion.
For there the Lord bestows his blessing, even life forevermore."
(Psalm 133:2-3)

In the Psalms of David, it is evident that the flow of the oil ultimately culminates in the blood of Jesus Christ, thus bestowing upon the individual the gift of eternal life.

The crucifixion of Jesus Christ was not the conclusion, but rather the inaugural moment of the establishment of the kingdom of God. As we celebrate the power of this remarkable "blood" in the sacraments of "bread and wine," our mission begins. We are able to engage in missionary work because, as the Book of Romans states, a righteous God has justified us, changing our status from that of sinners to that of missionaries.

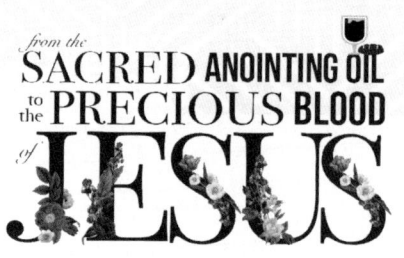

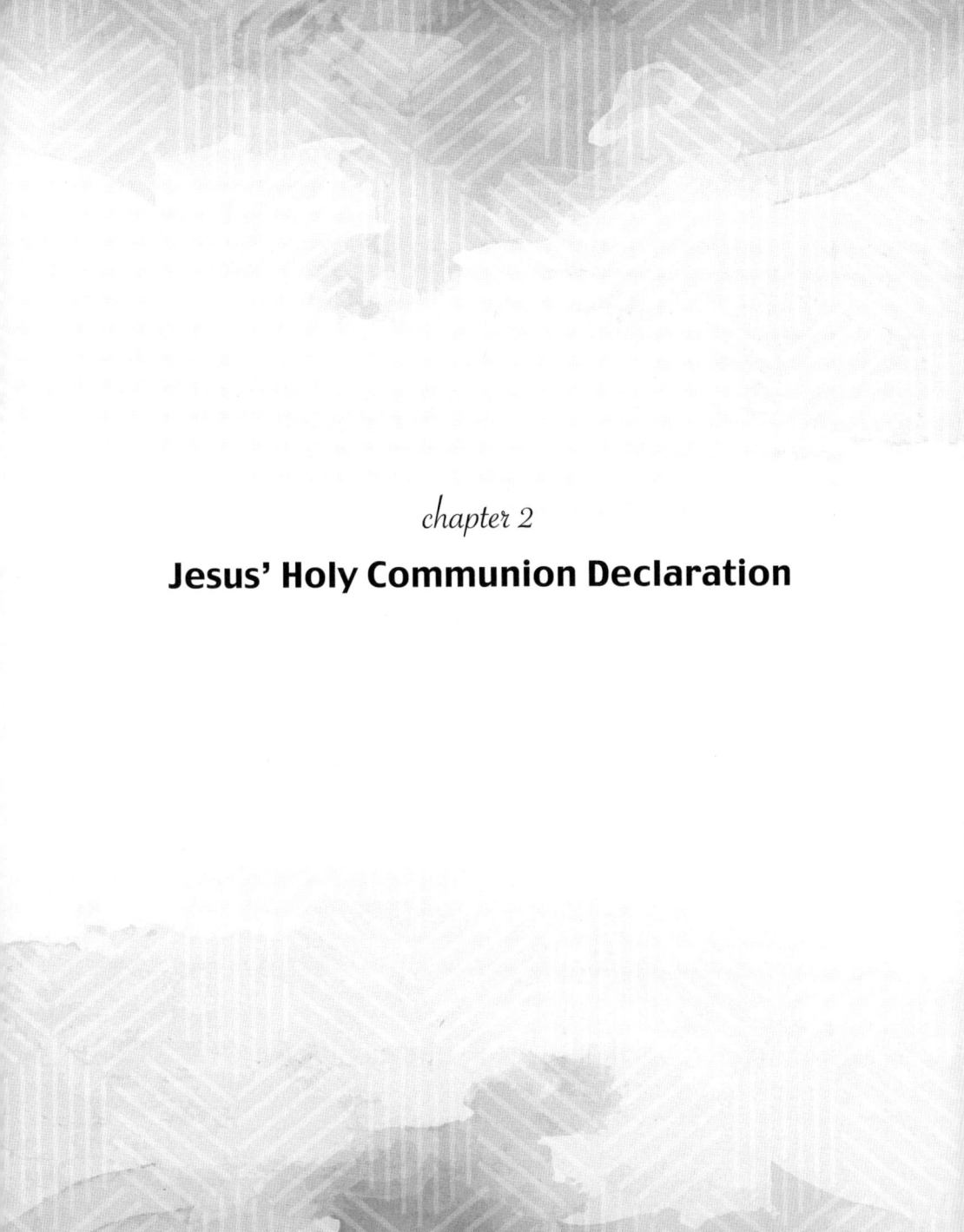

chapter 2

Jesus' Holy Communion Declaration

As we read the records of the 'last passover and first communion,' we need to be able to see the similarities between Matthew, Mark, and Luke, and John separately and at the same time as one story.

Jesus consumed bread and wine, which symbolized his flesh and blood, and stated, "Do this in remembrance of me," thereby establishing the "new covenant." Matthew, Mark, and Luke provide comprehensive accounts of this significant event, attesting to the fact that Jesus' incarnation and descent to Earth was for the purpose of atoning for our sins and offering his flesh and blood as a singular sacrifice on the cross.

The Apostle John, who had read all of Matthew, Mark, and Luke's accounts, wrote the Gospel of John many years later, focusing on the message that Jesus had delivered on that occasion. In other words, in terms of the ritual and the words, the Apostle John focused more on the words themselves. It is therefore necessary to consider the story of the Upper Room, or Jesus' final farewell message (John 13 through 17), and the Eucharist as recorded in the Synoptic Gospels of Matthew, Mark, and Luke as a whole.

Ultimately, the Synoptic Gospels and the Gospel of John present a unified account of the First Communion at the Last Passover. In the final Passover, Jesus established the first communion, thereby inaugurating the new covenant. This was done by commanding that his flesh and blood be commemorated in "bread and wine." In the subsequent account, as recorded in the Gospel of John, Jesus instructs his followers on how they should commemorate the Lord's Supper. He also informs them that they are not alone in this act of remembrance, but that they are accompanied by the Holy Spirit, also known as the Comforter.

It is important to distinguish between a declaration and a testimony. A declaration can be defined as a formal public statement made to the outside world. A testimony is a statement made by an individual who has observed and is therefore able to confirm the veracity of a fact. Accordingly, declarations are of primary importance, with testimony taking a secondary position. Following Jesus' proclamation, numerous testimonies were provided.

At the inaugural communion of the final Passover, Jesus made three declarations. Initially, he proclaimed the establishment of a "new covenant." Subsequently, he identified himself as a "Christian." Finally, he declared the presence of the Holy Spirit, also known as the Comforter. A review of the Bible reveals that God had been preparing for a considerable period of time for Jesus' three declarations at the Lord's Supper.

As Jesus indicates in the parable of the vine and the branches, Christians who are united with him will celebrate the Eucharist as witnesses to the new covenant. They will become "houses of the Holy Spirit," the dwelling place of the Holy Spirit whom Jesus will send, and will be guided by the Holy Spirit to live as glorified public servants of God's kingdom, fulfilling the Great Commission until Jesus returns. Jesus recounted this remarkable account at the First Supper of the Last Passover, and thus, it is imperative to consider the Synoptic Gospels and the Gospel of John, which document the events of that fateful day, as a unified whole.

 1

During the First Communion, Jesus declared the "New Covenant"

During the 'last passover and first communion,' Jesus declared the 'New Covenant.'

"And he took bread, gave thanks and broke it, and gave it to them, saying, "This is my body given for you; do this in remembrance of me." In the same way, after the supper he took the cup, saying,
"This cup is the new covenant in my blood, which is poured out for you." (Luke 22:19-20)

The New Covenant Established through the Flesh and Blood of Jesus

The concept of a "new covenant" is predicated on the Mosaic covenant of 1,500 years ago, which is also known as the Sinai covenant. Accordingly, an understanding of the Sinai covenant, which was established at Sinai under Moses, is a prerequisite to an examination of the words that gave rise to the new covenant as the Mosaic covenant became the old covenant.

"Moses then took the blood, sprinkled it on the people and said, "This is the blood of the covenant that the Lord has made with you in accordance with all these words." (Exodus 24:8)

The Sinai Covenant is the account of the Hebrew people's exodus from slavery in Egypt and their sojourn at Mount Sinai. During this period, with Moses acting as mediator, the people "sprinkle the blood of bulls on the altar representing God (Exodus 24:6) and on the people (Exodus 24:8), and make a holy civil covenant of a kingdom of priests." The essence of the Sinai Covenant can be defined as a covenant between God and the Hebrew people, the descendants of Abraham, in which the two parties agree upon the future relationship between them as a kingdom of priests.

The essence of the Sinai Covenant can be distilled into five principal elements. The initial component is the Ten Commandments, which represent a distilled version of the 613 laws. The second element is the tabernacle, which served as a symbol of God's presence and provided a setting for the priests and their ritual practices. Thirdly, there are the five sacrifices (burnt offerings, sin offerings, fellowship offerings, guilt offerings, and sin offerings). The fourth element is comprised of the three principal holidays observed by a kingdom of priests. These are Passover, the Feast of Tabernacles, and the Feast of Weeks. The fifth element is the three feasts of a kingdom of priests. The final category comprises the Sabbaths, Sabbaticals, and Jubilees.

The five primary tenets of the Mount Sinai covenant subsequently constituted the subsequent trajectory of the Israelites, who became "holy citizens of a kingdom of priests" through their entry into a priestly covenant with God. Should the Israelites adhere to this covenant, they will be bestowed with blessings, as the love of God and love of neighbor, as exemplified by the Law, will be actualized. Nevertheless, in the event of the Israelites' failure to uphold the terms of their covenant with God, they are subject to divine condemnation. The blessings and curses are contingent upon the Israelites' fulfillment of the covenant.

Furthermore, between the Sinai Covenant and the New Covenant, a "New Covenant Foreshadowing" is posited through Jeremiah.

"The days are coming," declares the Lord,
"when I will make a new covenant
with the people of Israel
and with the people of Judah.
⋯ "This is the covenant I will make with the people of Israel
after that time," declares the Lord.
"I will put my law in their minds
and write it on their hearts.
I will be their God,
and they will be my people." (Jeremiah 31:31-33)

The foundation of the Sinai Covenant served as the basis for the existence of a kingdom of priests for a period of 1,500 years. Furthermore, on the foundation of a kingdom of priests, Jesus proclaimed the new covenant at the first communion of the last Passover. The Sinai covenant, established by Moses with the blood of bulls, became the old covenant when Jesus declared, "A new covenant I establish with my blood." With the proclamation of the new covenant, the Mosaic covenant was effectively superseded and rendered obsolete. Those who maintain that the Mosaic covenant is still in effect are in a position of considerable difficulty. The establishment of a new covenant and the proclamation of a new promise are contingent upon the assumption that the previous covenant has reached its conclusion. The previous promises are still in effect, but are now superseded by the new covenant.

"Then he sent young Israelite men,
and they offered burnt offerings and sacrificed young bulls as fellowship offerings to the Lord.
Moses took half of the blood and put it in bowls,
and the other half he splashed against the altar.
Then he took the Book of the Covenant and read it to the people.
They responded,
"We will do everything the Lord has said; we will obey."
Moses then took the blood, sprinkled it on the people and said,
"This is the blood of the covenant that the Lord has made with you in accordance with all these words." (Exodus 24:5-8)

"Subsequently, after the evening repast, he performed the same rite with the cup, proclaiming,
"In the same way, after the supper he took the cup, saying,
"This cup is the new covenant in my blood,
which is poured out for you." (Luke 22:20)

Prior to the proclamation of the Old Covenant, as established at Mount Sinai, a period of three days was allotted for preparation. Ultimately, on the third day, God initiated the descent of the covenant by opening the gates of heaven and descending upon Mount Sinai. In His declaration of the Ten Commandments, God stated, "I am the Lord your God, who brought you out of the land of Egypt, out of the house of bondage" (Exodus 20:2). As God's pronouncements to the Israelites persisted, the populace, fearful of directly encountering the divine will, petitioned Moses to serve as an intermediary.

"Speak to us yourself and we will listen.
But do not have God speak to us or we will die." (Exodus 20:19)

The Israelites were too intimidated to persist in listening to God's pronouncement of the law, which is why they requested that Moses intercede on their behalf, motivated by feelings of fear, reverence, and other factors. However, the tone of Jesus' new covenant declaration in the first sacrament differed from that of the Sinai covenant. In order to gain a full understanding of the new covenant, it is essential to consider it in the context of the old covenant declaration.

The Sinai Covenant has been in effect for 1,500 years, which is why Jesus, at the age of twelve, accompanied by Mary and Joseph, undertook a journey from Nazareth to Jerusalem to observe the Passover holiday. Nevertheless, following Jesus' pronouncement of the New Covenant, it became unlawful to attend the Temple in Jerusalem to observe the Passover laws. With the proclamation of the new covenant, the five sacrificial rituals of the priestly nation—the Passover, the Feast of

the last supper | Jean-Baptiste de Champaigne 作

Tabernacles, the Feast of Weeks, the Sabbath, the Sabbatical year, and the Jubilee year—ceased to be observed.

Over the past 1,500 years, the "Law of the Land of the Priests" has endured despite the domination of various empires, including the Assyrian, Babylonian, Persian, and Hellenic. Even during the period when Judea was under the rule of the Roman Empire, the law of the priestly order remained centred in the Jerusalem Temple. Indeed, the Temple in Jerusalem became so commercialized that even Jews in the diaspora, who were scattered throughout the Roman Empire, would gather there to celebrate holidays according to the Law of the Temple. Consequently, 1,500 years of the Law of the Temple, encompassing all of its rituals, feasts, and holidays, reached its conclusion with Jesus' pronouncement of the New Covenant. It is important to consider the significance of the New Covenant as a pivotal declaration in religious history.

Jesus established the new covenant through the shedding of his flesh and blood. On that night, Jesus fulfilled the new covenant by being arrested by the Sanhedrin and shedding his blood on the cross of the Roman Empire. The old covenant represented God's justice, whereas the new covenant represents the consummation of that justice through the cross. This is a significant point. God proclaimed His justice 1,500 years ago at Mount Sinai. The realization of this proclamation is the New Covenant of Jesus. Let us examine this assertion in greater detail.

The term for this concept is as follows: The term "fellowship offering" is used in this context. God bestowed upon the Israelites, who were bound to Him by a priestly covenant, the priestly law, which demanded the shedding of blood as a prerequisite for His forgiveness of human sin.

For example, the Bible recounts that after Adam violated his covenant with God by sinning, he sought refuge from God among the trees in the Garden of Eden. God did not approach Adam and suggest that the incident be overlooked. Rather than punishing him, God forgave Adam for eating from the tree of the knowledge of good and evil, but he clothed him in skins and sent him out of the Garden of Eden. The act of God clothed Adam in animal skins was, in fact, a blood sacrifice.

The shedding of blood represented God's means of renewing his relationship with sinful human beings. The shedding of blood for the purpose of forgiveness was a necessary component of the process of reconciling sinful human beings with God. Thus, God's justice was repeatedly demonstrated through the shedding of blood. At the first Passover, the blood of a lamb was applied to the doorposts and lintel of the house. Similarly, at the covenant at Sinai, a bull was slain and its blood was sprinkled on the altar and on the people. Subsequently, human beings were able to stand before God through five rituals and five sacrifices, thereby obtaining forgiveness for their sins.

The five sacrifices were observed for a period of 1,500 years until Jesus Christ, in his role as the ultimate sacrifice, shed his blood on the cross to fulfill God's justice. The concept of forgiveness of sins is contingent upon the shedding of blood. The five sacrifices of a kingdom of priests are no longer necessary, as the one sacrifice of Jesus' blood on the cross is considered the "perfect sacrifice" before God. This is the fundamental premise of the "new covenant declaration" of the inaugural communion, which is extensively discussed in the Book of Hebrews.

"This is why even the first covenant was not put into effect without blood.
When Moses had proclaimed every command of the law to all the people, he took the blood of calves, together with water, scarlet wool and branches of hyssop, and sprinkled the scroll and all the people.
He said, "This is the blood of the covenant, which God has commanded you to keep."
In the same way, he sprinkled with the blood both the tabernacle and everything used in its ceremonies.
In fact, the law requires that nearly everything be cleansed with blood, and without the shedding of blood there is no forgiveness."
(Hebrews 9:18-22)

With regard to the crucifixion of Jesus, the Sanhedrin initially resolved to kill Jesus on this Passover. However, upon Jesus's arrival in Jerusalem and observation of the crowds cheering and shouting, "Hosanna, descendant of David," the Sanhedrin was so alarmed that they altered their initial plan and resolved once more to postpone the killing of Jesus on this Passover. Nevertheless, Jesus made it evident that he would be subjected to crucifixion during the Passover.

"As you know, the Passover is two days away—and the Son of Man will be handed over to be crucified." (Matthew 26:2)

Regardless of the capricious decisions of the Sanhedrin, Jesus proceeded to fulfill God's will on earth, as it is in heaven, in God's time. In light of Judas Iscariot's betrayal, the Sanhedrin once again reversed their decision and resolved to kill Jesus, this time on Passover. Upon examination of the sequence of events, it becomes evident that the term "Passover" is applicable in this context.

The concept of the "Passover lamb" provides a foundation for understanding the "Lamb of God." The blood of Jesus becomes the "blood of the covenant" when the narrative of the sprinkling of blood in the making of the covenant with Moses is understood. These events were part of a larger preparation for the moment of Jesus' arrival, which represented the manifestation of God's dispensational predestination in the fullness of time. Similarly, as God observed the blood of the lamb and spared the firstborn Hebrews during the Passover, so God observed the blood of Jesus and saved humanity. This represents the establishment of a new covenant between God and humanity. The blood of Jesus has effectively superseded the necessity for a blood covenant between God and humanity. The act of offering sacrifices with the blood of animals is rendered futile if one's intention is to make the cross or the blood of Jesus itself the basis for such an offering.

"While they were eating, Jesus took bread, and when he had given thanks, he broke it and gave it to his disciples, saying, "Take it; this is my body."
Then he took a cup, and when he had given thanks,
he gave it to them, and they all drank from it.

The Institution of the Eucharist or Jesus Christ instituting the Eucharist
Nicolas Poussin 作

· Jesus made a new covenant with his body and blood

Moses' Covenant of Mt. Sinai
(blood of a calf)

Then he sent young Israelite men, and they offered burnt offerings and sacrificed young bulls as fellowship offerings to the Lord. Moses took half of the blood and put it in bowls, and the other half he splashed against the altar. ⋯ Moses then took the blood, sprinkled it on the people and said, "This is the blood of the covenant that the Lord has made with you in accordance with all these words."(Exe 24:5-8)

Jesus' New Covenant
(Jesus' body and blood)

This is my body given for you
This cup is the new covenant in my blood, which is poured out for you.(Lk 22:19-20)

End of sacrificial laws, festival laws of a Kingdom of Priests

And he took bread, gave thanks and broke it, and gave it to them, saying,
This is my body given for you; do this in remembrance of me.
In the same way, after the supper he took the cup, saying,
This cup is the new covenant in my blood, which is poured out for you (Lk 22:19-20)

"This is my blood of the covenant, which is poured out for many," he said to them." (Mark 14:22-24)

The new covenant is not a reiteration of the covenant established at Mount Sinai; rather, it is a novel promise made by Jesus during his earthly ministry, which served to fulfill the covenant established at Mount Sinai. In contrast to the old covenant at Sinai, which was a practical process of fulfilling the future promise of a kingdom of priests, the new covenant represents Jesus' proclamation of the practical fulfillment of the future promise of the kingdom of God.

The New Covenant represents the inaugural chapter of God's future kingdom, comprising five fundamental elements.

First and foremost, the New Covenant offers the hope of resurrection and eternal life. Jesus died and subsequently rose from the dead as a singular, irrevocable sacrifice on the cross, thereby atoning for the sins of humanity. In consequence of his resurrection, Jesus became the first fruits of the resurrection, thereby inaugurating the hope of resurrection and eternal life for all Christians.

Secondly, the fulfillment of the Great Commission. Christians are uniquely positioned to fulfill the Great Commission, which is to disseminate the hope of resurrection and eternal life to all people. The Great Commission represents the substance of the New Covenant, which encompasses both the present and future narratives of the Kingdom of God. As Christians undertake the Great Commission, they are accompanied by the Comforter, the Holy Spirit, which Jesus will send.

Thirdly, the Christian's body is considered to be the temple of God and a conduit for the Holy Spirit. The concept of "your body becomes a temple" represents an extraordinary privilege and blessing bestowed upon Christians by God. It evokes the imagery of the Old Testament tabernacle and temple where God dwelt, and the profound assertion that the Holy Spirit resides within the Christian who is unified with Jesus.

Fourthly, the promise of Jesus' return. According to Christian doctrine, Jesus, having been resurrected and ascended, is seated at the right hand of God and will come in the clouds of heaven.

In conclusion, at the final judgment, Jesus will create a new heaven and a new earth, as well as a new Jerusalem, to which all of God's children will be invited.

These promises collectively represent the reality of the new covenant as espoused by Jesus, encompassing both the present and future of God's kingdom. As Christians, it is incumbent upon us to believe, hope, and live in accordance with this reality.

Symbolism of the Bread and Wine – Christian Communion

The Christian communion, symbolized by bread and wine, represents the "first Passover," which did not commence with a day that God designated as such. Instead, it originated with a significant practical action. In Egypt, 600,000 of the firstborn of the Israelites, descendants of Abraham, consumed three items: roasted meat from a year-old lamb, unleavened bread, and bitter herbs. They did so expeditiously, with sashes around their waists, shoes on their feet, and sticks in their hands. The dietary regimen observed during the inaugural Passover in Egypt has been replicated for 1,500 years, exhibiting minimal alteration over time. However, since the establishment of the New Covenant, Christians no longer consume the roasted meat of a year-old lamb, unleavened bread, and bitter herbs in observance of Passover. In lieu of the traditional roasted meat and unleavened bread, Christians are instructed to consume matzah (unleavened bread) and wine as a remembrance of the flesh and blood of Jesus.

One might inquire as to why Jesus chose to symbolize his flesh and blood with bread and wine for his twelve disciples at the last Passover. The rationale can be traced back to the incident of the high priest Melchizedek meeting Abraham.

"After Abram returned from defeating Kedorlaomer
and the kings allied with him, the king of Sodom came out to meet him in the Valley of Shaveh (that is, the King's Valley).
Then Melchizedek king of Salem brought out bread and wine.
He was priest of God Most High." (Genesis 14:17-18)

Upon Abraham's return from his successful military campaign, during which he rescued Lot, Melchizedek, the king of Salem, was awaiting his arrival. Melchizedek provided an interpretation of the reason for Abraham's previous night's victory.

- **Since Jesus established the New Covenant, Christians ate bread and wine in remembrance of Jesus' body and blood**

First Passover
meat of a one-year-old lamb,
unleavened bread,
bitter herbs

Last Passover
Bread and wine

After Abram returned from defeating Kedorlaomer and the kings allied with him, …
Then Melchizedek king of Salem brought out bread and wine.
He was priest of God Most High, and he blessed Abram, saying (Gen 14:17-18)

where our forerunner, Jesus, has entered on our behalf.
He has become a high priest forever, in the order of Melchizedek (Heb 6:20)

Abraham y Melquisedec | Juan Antonio de Frías y Escalante 作

"And praise be to God Most High,
who delivered your enemies into your hand."
Then Abram gave him a tenth of everything." (Genesis 14:20)

Melchizedek, the priest of God, informed Abraham that his victory in the war was due to God's assistance. In response to this interpretation, Abraham paid Melchizedek a tithe of the spoils of war. It is noteworthy that the bread and wine which Melchizedek had prepared on his way out to meet Abraham were consumed in this context.

"Then Melchizedek king of Salem brought out bread and wine.
He was priest of God Most High." (Genesis 14:18)

Melchizedek was a priest of the Most High God. The high priesthood of Jesus was not of the order of Aaron of the tribe of Levi, but rather of the order of Melchizedek. Jesus became an eternal high priest after the order of Melchizedek, offering his own blood as a sacrifice on the cross in the heavenly sanctuary.

"The Lord has sworn and will not change his mind:
"You are a priest forever, in the order of Melchizedek." (Psalm 110:4)

"Where our forerunner, Jesus, has entered on our behalf.
He has become a high priest forever, in the order of Melchizedek."
(Hebrews 6:20)

The high priesthood originated with Aaron of the tribe of Levi. However, over five centuries prior to Aaron's appointment as the inaugural high priest of a kingdom of priests, his forefather Abraham had paid tithes to God's priest Melchizedek and been bestowed with bread and wine. Jesus does not follow in the footsteps of Aaron, the visible high priest, but rather goes beyond that. Consequently, he follows in the footsteps of Melchizedek, who has no beginning and no end. The bread and wine that Melchizedek brought out are used to bless Abraham as a symbol of blessing to commemorate him.

From 'Celebrate this Day' to 'Celebrate Me'

The term "commemorate" is of significant importance. It signifies the act of bestowing significance upon an event that has marked a pivotal moment in the past and maintaining its relevance in the present. The past is the period of time that has elapsed, the present is the current moment, and the future is the period of time that is yet to come. The term "commemorate" is employed to integrate the past, present, and future. Consequently, when an event from the past is commemorated, it is done for the present, but it is also conveyed to the future. To illustrate, a person's birthday is often celebrated. The celebration and commemoration of a person's past, present, and future are collectively observed on the occasion of their birthday. Similarly, national anniversaries serve to reintroduce past events to the present and to open up the future, thereby encouraging collective action to improve the future. Such commemorations thus become the defining identity of the country.

Furthermore, commemoration serves as a primary mode of governance. In the Bible, the language of memorialization is employed to encompass

- **Since Jesus established the New Covenant, Christians can celebrate Jesus in any place and at any time**

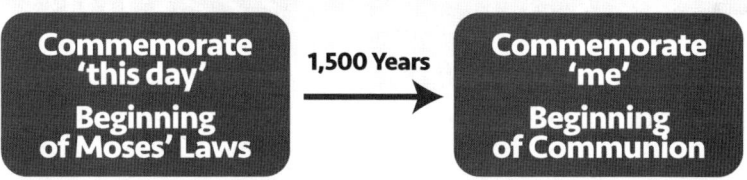

Do this in remembrance of me(Lk 22:19) - Repeatedly commemorating with bread and wine

Baptism and Holy Communion
: A system that makes it possible to carry out the Great Commission to the ends of the earth

And he took bread, gave thanks and broke it, and gave it to them, saying,
This is my body given for you; do this in remembrance of me (Lk 22:19)

the past, present, and future, thereby establishing a language of divine rule. In order to govern the world, God employed the concept of the memorial, encompassing the past, present, and future, as a means of perpetuating His reign.

In the context of the Hebrew people's initial Passover experience, God instructed them to 'remember this day.' From this 'day,' the Feast of Tabernacles, Pentecost, and Sukkot derive.

"This is a day you are to commemorate;
for the generations to come you shall celebrate it as a festival
to the Lord—a lasting ordinance." (Exodus 12:14)

It is noteworthy that Jesus transformed Passover, a 1,500-year-old celebration of a kingdom of priests, into a communion celebration of the individual self. He transformed the Old Testament Passover from a commemoration of a specific day among 365 in the annual cycle to a celebration of the individual. Moreover, he introduced the Eucharist into the world, thereby enabling all to live in the future as one in the person of Jesus. The celebration of the Eucharist marked a significant turning point.

"And he took bread, gave thanks and broke it,
and gave it to them, saying,
"This is my body given for you;
do this in remembrance of me." (Luke 22:19)

Jesus instituted the first communion by taking bread and wine and saying, "Do this in remembrance of me." Prior to that time, each of the five sacrifices—burnt offerings, grain offerings, fellowship offerings, guilt offerings, and sin offerings—required a specific form to be completed. However, following Jesus' first communion, all previous ceremonial forms were superseded, and the subsequent celebration was to be of the same form, namely "bread and wine." It is evident that there is no alternative method for the repeated celebration of Jesus' flesh and blood apart from the sacrament of bread and wine, which Jesus himself established.

If the Passover "Remember this day" was the inaugural decree of the law established 1,500 years ago, then the words "Remember me" represent the genesis of the sacraments. The Bible provides insight into the sacrificial nature of Jesus' death on the cross, which was intended to save humanity. In this way, Jesus became a living sacrifice, also known as the Lamb of God. It is imperative that this remarkable occurrence be continually commemorated; however, it is also evident that reflection on this event would be impossible without the establishment of the bread and wine sacrament system by Jesus. The bread and wine sacrament system, which was established by Jesus when he said, "Remember me," provides an opportunity for reflection, appreciation, and rejoicing on a continual basis.

The sacrament instituted by Jesus was not a one-time event, but rather a memorial of the kingdom of God to be observed perpetually. Alternatively stated, it was to serve as a proclamation of the Lord's death until his return.

"For whenever you eat this bread and drink this cup,
you proclaim the Lord's death until he comes." (1 Corinthians 11:26)

The death of Jesus on the cross, his subsequent resurrection, ascension, and second coming are all encompassed within the phrase "commemorating the Lord's death." This is what Paul meant when he stated that he had elected to be solely acquainted with the concept of the cross (1 Corinthians 2:1-2). In this way, the concepts of 'the cross' and 'the Lord's Supper' are not distinct entities, but rather, they are one and the same. Similarly, the Passover celebration commemorated a kingdom of priests; thus, the Lord's Supper has become a commemoration of the kingdom of God. In this way, the Lord's Supper is another blessing bestowed upon humanity, and it is a celebration that must be observed and recounted repeatedly until the Lord's return.

Consequently, baptism and the Lord's Supper represent the two principal ordinances that have facilitated the implementation of the Great Commission across the globe. The Lord's Supper has been observed widely and effectively for two millennia, conferring blessings upon all Christians.

In consequence of Jesus' declaration of the New Covenant, Christians have been enabled to celebrate Jesus through the Lord's Supper, not on any particular day or place, but 'at any time and in any place.' In a kingdom of priests, Passover was celebrated on a fixed date and in a designated location, which was deemed sacred by God. This was a law pertaining to the priestly order that had to be observed without any deviation.

"Three times a year all your men must appear
before the Lord your God at the place he will choose:
at the Festival of Unleavened Bread,
the Festival of Weeks and the Festival of Tabernacles.
No one should appear before the Lord empty-handed:" (Deuteronomy 16:16)

When we consider the significant efforts made by numerous individuals to adhere to this law, it is encouraging to note that the New Covenant has facilitated the ability to partake in communion at any desired time and location. In light of these considerations, it is evident that Jesus' declaration of communion is a significant and profound one. In the absence of this declaration, the necessity for annual travel to Jerusalem would persist. However, the declaration of communion by Jesus enables Christians to commemorate his sacrifice by partaking in the ritual of eating and drinking bread and wine at any time and in any location.

 2

During the First Passover, Jesus made the 'Christian' Declaration

Jesus utilized the metaphor of the vine to assert that those who are unified with him are 'Christians,' analogous to the stem and branches of a vine.

"I am the true vine,
and my Father is the gardener.
He cuts off every branch in me that bears no fruit,
while every branch that does bear fruit he prunes
so that it will be even more fruitful.
You are already clean because of the word I have spoken to you.
Remain in me, as I also remain in you.
No branch can bear fruit by itself;
it must remain in the vine.
Neither can you bear fruit unless you remain in me." (John 15:1-4)

Christ the True Vine icon | 16th century

The Parable of the Vine: Christians unified with Jesus

What is a Christian? A Christian is defined as an individual who adheres to the teachings of Christ and acknowledges Him as the Messiah. Christians are disciples of Jesus, children of God, and people who love one another in accordance with the love of Christ.

The term 'Christian' is first attested in the writings of the church in Antioch.

"Then Barnabas went to Tarsus to look for Saul,
and when he found him, he brought him to Antioch.
So for a whole year Barnabas and Saul met with the church
and taught great numbers of people.
The disciples were called Christians first at Antioch." (Acts 11:25-26)

However, the term "Christian" did not emerge spontaneously within the church in Antioch. The term "Christian" originated from Jesus's "Christian proclamation" at the first communion, as illustrated in the parable of the vine. In the parable of the vine, Jesus elucidated that the farmer represents God, the vine signifies Jesus Christ, and the branches symbolize the disciples, or Christians—those who adhere to Christ. In this way, a connection is established between Jesus and his followers.

"I am the vine; you are the branches. If you remain in me and I in you, you will bear much fruit; apart from me you can do nothing." (John 15:5)

Those who adhere to the Christian faith are unified with Christ, the vine, in a manner analogous to the union between the vine and its branches. Those who adhere to the Christian faith are individuals who have been embraced by the sacrificial love of Jesus Christ, and, as a result, are regarded as brothers and sisters in Christ who demonstrate love and compassion for one another. In John 15:12, Jesus elucidated the essence of Christian identity when he stated, "My command is this: Love each other as I have loved you"

The commandment "Love one another" represents the core tenet of Christian love, as espoused by Jesus Christ and embodied in the Old Testament law of the Sinai Covenant. This covenant encapsulates the notion of divine love and the love of one's neighbor.

As a result of embracing the identity that Jesus espoused, namely, "You too shall love one another," Christians are able to extend the same love they have received from Jesus to their neighbors. This enables them to move beyond the confines of the narrative of Jesus' love and apply it to the broader context of their relationships with others. The act of loving one's neighbors can be seen as an extension of the Great Commission, which calls for the dissemination of love to all nations and to the furthest reaches of the earth until Jesus' return.

The parable of the vine, which features the image of wine, is found in the Old Testament. Let us briefly examine these examples.

In the context of the Old Testament, the three main fruit trees in Canaan, the Promised Land, are the olive tree, the fig tree, and the vine. Canaan is a land with minimal precipitation and a scarcity of

- During the First Communion,
  Jesus used the parable of the vine
  and declared that those who are one with Jesus are Christians,
  just as the vine trunk and branches are one

Parable of the vine — Farmer-God, Vine trunk-Jesus, Branch-Christians

- Three Fruits of Canaan: Grape, Olive, Apricot
- Symbol of Israel as a kingdom of priests, symbol of peace and prosperity
    - Noah, a man of the soil, proceeded to plant a vineyard.(Gen 9:20)
    - May God give you heaven's dew and earth's richness—an abundance of grain and new wine.(Gen 27:28)
    - During Solomon's lifetime Judah and Israel, from Dan to Beersheba, lived in safety,
      everyone under their own vine and under their own fig tree.(1 ki 4:25)
- In the Kingdom of God,
  one can enjoy the blessings of 'being a Christian' through the wine of the Eucharist,
  which symbolizes the precious blood of Jesus

Isaac Blessing Jacob | Nicolas-Guy Brenet 作

surface water. However, the presence of dew allows for the growth of plants that can withstand the arid conditions, particularly those with the capacity to establish deep root systems. This made it an optimal environment for the cultivation of olives, figs, and grapes. These trees, which flourished throughout the land, served as emblems of Israel. The profusion of their fruits became a symbol of Israel's peace and prosperity.

The earliest known reference to the vine appears in the biblical record, in the story of Noah.

The narrative of Noah planting a vineyard was a symbol of divine favor following the deluge. God bestowed upon Noah and his descendants the blessing of "be fruitful and multiply and replenish the earth," and Noah, in turn, planted a vine and initiated the practice of agriculture.

"Noah, a man of the soil, proceeded to plant a vineyard." (Genesis 9:20)

From this point onward, the narrative progresses with the planting of a vine in the aftermath of the flood, which signifies the recovery and regeneration of the land.

The narrative of wine emerges in the account of Jacob receiving the blessing of his father Isaac. Following Abraham's journey from Ur of the Chaldees through Harran and eventual settlement in Canaan, the land that God had promised him, Abraham's son Isaac also established a presence in Canaan. As the years passed and Isaac's time drew near, he instructed his son Esau to hunt and procure a delicacy for him to bless him before his demise. Upon hearing the story, Rebekah, Isaac's wife, sent meat and wine to her husband, Isaac, with the intention of securing Jacob's inheritance over Esau's. Subsequently, Isaac, having mistaken Jacob for Esau, consumed the meat Jacob had brought, imbibed the wine, and bestowed a blessing upon Jacob.

"May God give you heaven's dew and earth's richness—
an abundance of grain and new wine.
May nations serve you and peoples bow down to you.
Be lord over your brothers,
and may the sons of your mother bow down to you.
May those who curse you be cursed
and those who bless you be blessed." (Genesis 27:28-29)

Isaac bestowed a blessing upon Jacob, stating, "May I give thee an abundance of grain and wine." Isaac's blessing illustrates the significance of wine as a symbol of profound blessing.

Wine is referenced once more in the account of the vine during the reign of Solomon.

"During Solomon's lifetime Judah and Israel, from Dan to Beersheba, lived in safety, everyone under their own vine
and under their own fig tree." (1 Kings 4:25)

During the reign of Solomon as King of Israel, it was asserted that the entire nation, from Dan to Beersheba, enjoyed peace and prosperity under the protection of their own vines and fig trees. This assertion serves to illustrate the notion that every household in Israel was a recipient of divine blessing.

During the course of his public ministry, Jesus performed his first miracle utilising wine. Miracles represent a means of divine control that transcends the laws of cause and effect. A review of the life of Jesus reveals that he performed and demonstrated numerous miracles during his public ministry. The initial miracle performed by Jesus occurred at a wedding feast in Cana of Galilee.

"Jesus said to the servants, "Fill the jars with water";
so they filled them to the brim.
Then he told them,
"Now draw some out and take it to the master of the banquet."
They did so, and the master of the banquet tasted the water that had been turned into wine.
He did not realize where it had come from,
though the servants who had drawn the water knew.
Then he called the bridegroom aside and said,
"Everyone brings out the choice wine first and then the cheaper wine after the guests have had too much to drink; but you have saved the best till now."
What Jesus did here in Cana of Galilee was the first of the signs through which he revealed his glory; and his disciples believed in him."
(John 2:7-11)

The first miracle attributed to Jesus was the transformation of water into wine. However, some scholars posit that this miracle was a

The wedding at Cana | Denys Calvaert 作

· Jesus' first miracle and the first Communion

**First miracle:
wedding feast at Cana**
Turning water into wine

First Communion
Commemorating the precious
blood of Jesus with wine

What Jesus did here in Cana of Galilee was the first of the signs through which he revealed his glory;
and his disciples believed in him (Jn 2:11)

and the master of the banquet tasted the water that had been turned into wine. He did not realize
where it had come from, though the servants who had drawn the water knew (Jn 2:9)

This is my body given for you; do this in remembrance of me
This cup(wine cup) is the new covenant in my blood, which is poured out for you (Lk 22:19-20)

precursor to an even more remarkable event: the "wine" consumed during the first communion at the Last Supper. The early Church Fathers engaged in debate regarding the symbolism of the wine in question, particularly whether it represented the blood of Jesus. Of greater significance to our comprehension of the entirety of the Bible than the aforementioned debates is the fact that the wine which Jesus provided for commemoration symbolizes the "blood" of Jesus. In offering the wine and declaring, "This cup is the new covenant in my blood, which is poured out for you" (Luke 22:20), Jesus performed a miracle that is unparalleled in magnitude and significance. It is a miracle that transcends the boundaries of imagination and serves as a profound symbol of the greatest blessing.

While the miracle of the wedding feast at Cana was experienced by only a select few, the first communion marks the inception of an extraordinary phenomenon that has been witnessed by all of humanity throughout the course of history. In this way, Christians may partake of the 'riches and blessings of Christianity' through the consumption of the wine that symbolizes the blood of Jesus in the Lord's Supper. The blessings of heaven are bestowed upon Christians.

Jesus' parable of the vine does not merely advocate financial stability; it extends beyond that to encompass a holistic approach to life. The pinnacle of Christian abundance is to become a person of Jesus. This is made evident by the parable of the vine. In essence, Jesus' teachings indicate that one can be a Christian by becoming attached to the vine and uniting with it. The phrase "Remain in me, as I also remain in you" (John 15:4) signifies that Jesus dwells in the Christian who has consumed his flesh and drunk his blood. Christians are instructed to abide in Jesus as a perpetual reminder of this. The Apostle Paul further elucidated this concept in his writings, stating, "I no longer live, but Christ lives in me" (Galatians 2:20). The Christian proclamation originated with this significant sacrament.

Christians – Public Servants of the Kingdom of God

An additional interpretation of the 'Christian' declaration made by Jesus at the Lord's Supper is that of a 'public servant of the Kingdom of God.' In Israel following the Sinai Covenant, the Levites constituted the priesthood, but by extension, all men over the age of 20 who were fit for military service were also considered priesthood officers. In the Eucharist, Jesus states that Christians are public servants in the kingdom of God.

In the context of the Last Supper, Jesus made a remark that is often interpreted as a foreshadowing of the betrayal of Judas Iscariot. He stated that the hand of the one who would sell him was present at the table. The disciples then inquired of one another as to the identity of the individual who would perpetrate such an act. An altercation then arose among the disciples, with each contending that they were the greatest. Upon realizing that his disciples were engaged in a futile debate regarding the relative merits of greatness, Jesus intervened to halt the discussion. In lieu of this, he informed them of the immense value he placed on their relationship, having spent the previous three years in close proximity.

"You are those who have stood by me in my trials." (Luke 22:28)

The disciples of Jesus had been his 'comrades, companions, and co-laborers' in the course of his public ministry over the previous three years. The disciples had accompanied Jesus during all of his public appearances and had been present with him during all of his trials and sufferings. In recognition of their loyalty and support, Jesus offered them this remarkable testament: "You are those who have stood by me in my trials" (Luke 22:28). In other words, to Jesus, the disciples were the most valuable and appreciated co-workers, the most dedicated public servants of God's kingdom, and those who were most worthy of esteem. In this way, Jesus taught that the debate about who is the greatest is meaningless. All public servants of God's kingdom are of equal standing and importance, each fulfilling a distinct and essential role.

Subsequently, Jesus made an even more noteworthy pronouncement to his disciples: just as God had bestowed the kingdom of God upon his son Jesus, so now Jesus proclaimed that he would bestow the kingdom of God upon his disciples. In a similar manner to how Jesus, the 'Savior,' assumed control of the kingdom of God as the 'Anointed One,' the Messiah (Christ), his disciples would subsequently assume control of the mission of God's public office as Christians.

"And I confer on you a kingdom,
just as my Father conferred one on me,
so that you may eat and drink at my table
in my kingdom and sit on thrones,
judging the twelve tribes of Israel." (Luke 22:29-30)

In a previous instance, John the Baptist had introduced the concept of the kingdom of God, declaring, "Repent, for the kingdom of heaven has come near" (Matthew 3:2). Subsequently, Jesus would fulfill the new covenant through his death on the cross and complete the kingdom of God by uniting a kingdom of priests. He stated that he was bestowing the kingdom of God upon his disciples. The act of entrusting the kingdom entails the designation of the disciples as officers within it. All who consume the flesh and blood of Jesus become 'Christians' and are designated as officials of the kingdom of God, rather than a select few. A distinction may be made between the roles of those who eat the flesh and drink the blood of Jesus and those who do not, but there is no differentiation between those who are considered high and those who are considered low. In the Sermon on the Mount, Jesus states that all who consume his flesh and blood are Christians and thus become officials of the kingdom of God.

Subsequently, Jesus informed his disciples that he would facilitate their participation in the kingdom of God, wherein they would be seated on thrones and preside over the twelve tribes of Israel. He was indicating that, just as Jesus had completed his work on the cross by setting the example and obeying God's word to the end, and would sit at the right hand of God's throne and rule as the 'victorious ones,' so too would his twelve disciples become 'victors' by preaching the gospel for the sake of the kingdom of God, obeying it to the end, even to the point of death. He stated that the 'victors,' the ultimate triumphant individuals, would subsequently be invited to sit with Jesus on his throne, emulating Jesus' own triumph and seating himself with him on the throne of God.

"To the one who is victorious,
I will give the right to sit with me on my throne,
just as I was victorious and sat down with my Father on his throne."
(Revelation 3:21)

Subsequently, the Apostle John encountered Jesus on the Isle of Patmos and attested that

"and has made us to be a kingdom and priests to serve his God
and Father—to him be glory and power for ever and ever! Amen."
(Revelation 1:6)

It is only through an understanding of the public concept of a 'kingdom' that one can ascertain whether they have been made 'a kingdom and priests." The Bible, as a sacred text, contains a number of significant blessings, which were divinely bestowed upon humanity.

The question thus arises as to the identity of a 'Christian' who is an official in the kingdom of God, and the duration of their tenure in such a position. In response to this, Jesus stated that a 'Christian' is an individual who awaits the Second Coming while fulfilling Jesus' great commission and has been granted eternal life.

"For you granted him authority over all people that he might give eternal life to all those you have given him.
Now this is eternal life: that they know you, the only true God,
and Jesus Christ, whom you have sent." (John 17:2-3)

- **During the First Communion,
  Jesus declared that Christians can ask
  and receive anything when they live in Jesus**

I am the vine; you are the branches. If you remain in me and I in you,
you will bear much fruit; apart from me you can do nothing (Jn 15:5)

If you remain in me and my words remain in you,
ask whatever you wish, and it will be done for you (Jn 15:7)

A Kingdom of Priests	Forgiveness through a priest
The Kingdom of God	Christians can ask for forgiveness directly as a Priestly nation

"Therefore go and make disciples of all nations,
baptizing them in the name of the Father
and of the Son and of the Holy Spirit,
and teaching them to obey everything I have commanded you.
And surely I am with you always, to the very end of the age."
(Matthew 28:19-20)

"Men of Galilee," they said,
"why do you stand here looking into the sky?
This same Jesus, who has been taken from you into heaven,
will come back in the same way you have seen him go into heaven."
(Acts 1:11)

'Eternal life' is a gift from God to Christians through Jesus Christ. The knowledge of the living God and Jesus Christ is tantamount to eternal life.

Christians – Whatever you desire

At the first communion, Jesus stated that if a Christian remains in the Lord's grace, they may petition for anything and it shall be granted.

"I am the vine; you are the branches. If you remain in me and I in you, you will bear much fruit; apart from me you can do nothing." (John 15:5)

A Christian is defined as an individual who is capable of bearing significant spiritual fruit when they maintain a state of spiritual connection with Jesus. Conversely, when this connection is disrupted, the individual is rendered incapable of spiritual growth. The condition 'If he abides in me and I in him…' constitutes a promise of the following:

"If you remain in me and my words remain in you,
ask whatever you wish, and it will be done for you." (John 15:7)

In stating that "apart from me you can do nothing," Jesus was alluding to the fact that a branch cannot survive independently of the vine. This indicates that the identity of a Christian is in question. A Christian is defined as an individual who adheres to the teachings of Jesus and incorporates them into their daily life. It is therefore imperative that we undertake a detailed study of the Four Gospels.

The Four Gospels contain numerous sayings of Jesus, as well as numerous quotations from the Old Testament. Jesus frequently employs the phrase "It is written" in his quotations from the Old Testament. In order to gain an accurate understanding of the words of Jesus as recorded in the Four Gospels, it is first necessary to study the 39 books of the Old Testament. This is followed by an examination of the Four Gospels, after which the aim is to become a person of Jesus. This enables the individual to live the Christian life. Subsequently, one becomes established in the teachings of Jesus, and his words become a part of one's being. This enables one to request whatever one desires and receive it. This is the promise that Jesus made to Christians.

The phrase 'whatever you desire' indicates that there are no constraints on what humans can aspire to achieve. In a kingdom of priests, forgiveness could be requested through the presentation of a sacrifice, with the assistance of a priest. Consequently, the priest served as a conduit of divine favor and a public servant bearing a grave obligation.

In the kingdom of God, Christians are regarded as kings and priests, with the ability to seek forgiveness directly from God and to request whatever they desire. Each Christian has become a conduit for substantial blessings.

Christians are expected to conduct themselves in a manner that brings glory to God, through the act of petitioning for their desires and the production of spiritual fruit. Prayer is an integral aspect of Christian theology, and its practice is inextricably linked with the glorification of God.

"This is to my Father's glory, that you bear much fruit,
showing yourselves to be my disciples." (John 15:8)

As a disciple and follower of Jesus, one must adhere to the tenets of the Christian faith, which includes the belief in Jesus' atonement on the cross and the observance of the Lord's Supper. The latter is considered the most sacred aspect of the Christian tradition, and it is celebrated and observed throughout the lifespan of a believer. This ritual involves the consumption of bread and wine, which symbolizes the indwelling presence of Jesus and his teachings within the individual.

 3

During the First Communion, Jesus declared the coming of the "Holy Spirit"

During the First Communion of the Last Passover, Jesus declared that he would request that the Father send the Comforter, the Holy Spirit, to abide with humanity perpetually.

"And I will ask the Father, and he will give you another advocate to help you and be with you forever" (John 14:16)

Immanuel through the Holy Spirit

The Greek word for 'Comforter' is 'Parakletos' (one who is called to come alongside), which refers to the Holy Spirit. The term is used to signify various roles, including comforter, advocate, intercessor, and helper. Indeed, the Holy Spirit was present with Jesus for three years of his public ministry.

- **During the First Communion,
  Jesus declared that he will ask the Father
  to send the Holy Spirit to reside with us forever**

When being baptized

As soon as Jesus was baptized, he went up out of the water.
At that moment heaven was opened,
and he saw the Spirit of God descending like a dove and alighting on him.(Mat 3:16)

When being tested by Satan in the desert

Then Jesus was led by the Spirit into the wilderness
to be tempted by the devil.(Mat 4:1)

When Jesus was baptized by John, the Holy Spirit was with him.

"As soon as Jesus was baptized, he went up out of the water.
At that moment heaven was opened,
and he saw the Spirit of God descending like a dove
and alighting on him." (Matthew 3:16)

And when Jesus was tested by Satan in the desert, the Holy Spirit was with him.

"Then Jesus was led by the Spirit into the wilderness
to be tempted by the devil." (Matthew 4:1)

Jesus' public ministry was characterized by the presence of the Holy Spirit. However, the Holy Spirit, also known as the Comforter, was not yet present with the disciples until Jesus spoke of the Holy Spirit at the first communion, which took place at the last Passover. In this way, Jesus made the promise that the Holy Spirit would be sent to the disciples, and that this gift would be theirs forever. The concept of "Immanuel," or "God with us," is a central tenet of Christianity. In the New Testament, Jesus is identified as the embodiment of this divine presence. In addition to Jesus, the entity known as Immanuel, or "God with us," is now accompanied by the Holy Spirit.

When and Where the Holy Spirit will reside

The Holy Spirit will come to the disciples after Jesus' crucifixion, death, resurrection, and ascension. Jesus will pray to God at the right hand of God. The Holy Spirit will then come to the disciples. Accordingly, Jesus stated, "All this I have spoken while still with you" (John 14:25). It is significant to note that God will send the Holy Spirit, the Comforter, in Jesus' name after Jesus has completed his public ministry.

"But very truly I tell you, it is for your good that I am going away.
Unless I go away, the Advocate will not come to you;
but if I go, I will send him to you." (John 16:7)

The timing of the Holy Spirit's arrival is unambiguous: it occurred after Jesus' resurrection, subsequent 40-day stay on Earth, pronouncement of the Great Commission, and ascension into heaven. Jesus made this clear when the Comforter, the Holy Spirit, would come at the first communion, which is why Jesus said, 'It is good for you to go away.' In establishing the temporal and spatial parameters, Jesus indicated that the Comforter would arrive 'to you' following his own departure.

This raises the question of where the Holy Spirit dwells. The Holy Spirit dwells within the Christian community. In the Old Testament, a kingdom of priests served as a conduit for God's glory, which was primarily manifested within the tabernacle and temple. In accordance with the blueprint provided to Moses by God, Bezalel, Oholiab, Ithamar, and numerous other individuals collaborated to construct the tabernacle. Upon completion of the tabernacle, Moses conducted a final inspection. Subsequently, all components were installed, including the Ark of the Covenant within the tabernacle, the paving of the courtyard surrounding the tabernacle and altar, the hanging of the veil on the courtyard door, the completion of the work, and the dedication of the

- **During the First Communion, Jessus declared that after his ascension, the Holy Spirit will reside among Christians**

Point of Holy Spirit's dwelling	After Jesus' ascension
Place of Holy Spirit's dwelling	Christians

(cf. God's glory dwelling in the Tabernacle and the Temple)

> But very truly I tell you, it is for your good that I am going away Unless I go away, the Advocate will not come to you; but if I go, I will send him to you (Jn 16:7)

tabernacle. A cloud overshadowed the tabernacle, and the glory of God filled the tabernacle. This was the manner in which God manifested His presence.

The entire nation of Israel was present at the dedication of the tabernacle, where they experienced the presence of God's glory. This was subsequently reaffirmed at the first offering of Aaron, the high priest, on the eighth day of the priesthood commissioning ceremony.

"Then Aaron lifted his hands toward the people and blessed them.
And having sacrificed the sin offering,
the burnt offering and the fellowship offering, he stepped down.
Moses and Aaron then went into the tent of meeting.
When they came out, they blessed the people;
and the glory of the Lord appeared to all the people.
Fire came out from the presence of the Lord
and consumed the burnt offering and the fat portions on the altar.
And when all the people saw it,
they shouted for joy and fell facedown." (Leviticus 9:22-24)

Upon observing this phenomenon, the entire populace was overcome with awe and fell prostrate. In the days of Solomon, the glory of God was present in the newly constructed Temple in Jerusalem. This was evidenced by a cloud that descended when the Ark of the Covenant was placed within the temple precincts and by fire that consumed the temple at its dedication. The entire populace was thus able to experience the presence of God's glory.

"When the priests withdrew from the Holy Place,
the cloud filled the temple of the Lord.
And the priests could not perform their service because of the cloud,
for the glory of the Lord filled his temple." (1 Kings 8:10-11)

"When Solomon finished praying, fire came down from heaven
and consumed the burnt offering and the sacrifices,
and the glory of the Lord filled the temple.
The priests could not enter the temple
of the Lord because the glory of the Lord filled it." (2 Chronicles 7:1-2)

The construction of altars at Bethel and Dan by Jeroboam of Northern Israel for the purposes of sacrifice and incense burning resulted in the absence of divine presence. This was the law of a kingdom of priests that God had established. The term 'presence' denotes a state of being present, or in other words, of coming and dwelling. The accounts of God's presence in the Old Testament are invaluable for elucidating the concept of the Holy Spirit.

This foundation was the basis for Jesus's earthly ministry, which spanned three years and included public teachings, the crucifixion, and the first Eucharist, during which he proclaimed the presence of the Holy Spirit, also known as the Comforter. It is noteworthy that Jesus made the remarkable and significant declaration that the Holy Spirit is present in the Christian, not in a particular location on earth.

The Role of the Holy Spirit

It is evident that the significant pronouncements made by Jesus at the first communion following the Last Supper are inextricably linked to the crucifixion. The function of the Holy Spirit of Truth is to "testify" that healing has occurred as a result of Jesus' crucifixion, which entailed being nailed to the cross and having his flesh torn. The high priestly faction of the Sanhedrin derisively urged Jesus to descend from the cross. From their perspective, Jesus of Nazareth had proclaimed himself to be the Messiah and was subsequently executed. However, the crucifixion was the true work of the Messiah, and it is the Holy Spirit who testifies to this fact. The function of the Holy Spirit is to facilitate the revelation of this truth.

The phrase 'anointing of the Holy Spirit' is a popular one, even when repeated frequently. The anointing of the Holy Spirit, the leading of the Holy Spirit, praying, and the practice of calling out "Lord, Lord" appear to manifest in remarkable ways. However, these phenomena should not be regarded as the primary focus. It is essential to gain an understanding of the manner and timing of the Holy Spirit's arrival and the functions it fulfills upon doing so, as documented in the Bible.

Rather than studying the work of the Holy Spirit from the phenomenon of the Pentecostal event of the Descent of the Holy Spirit, it would be more beneficial to learn and know the work of the Holy Spirit from Jesus' declaration at the First Communion of the Last Passover. This is because it is from Jesus' declaration that the presence of the Holy Spirit begins.

At the First Communion, Jesus proffered an advance indication of the function of the Holy Spirit upon His arrival.

Primarily, the Holy Spirit, also known as the Comforter, serves to educate and remind individuals of the teachings and messages conveyed by Jesus.

"But the Advocate, the Holy Spirit,
whom the Father will send in my name,
will teach you all things and will remind you of everything
I have said to you." (John 14:26)

The Holy Spirit would serve as a conduit of knowledge, imparting teachings and reminders of significant events in Jesus' life, including his birth, three-year public ministry, crucifixion, resurrection, and the Great Commission. Jesus informed his disciples of this information in advance because the Sanhedrin, the persecutors of Jesus at the time, would persecute his disciples and impede his work for the kingdom of God after his crucifixion. Furthermore, the Sanhedrin Jews, who asserted that persecuting Jesus and his disciples was God's will, would be unlikely to accept the accounts of Jesus' disciples as truth.

However, Jesus' disciples were tasked with bearing witness to him in Jerusalem, Judea, Samaria, and to the ends of the earth. This was to be done despite the opposition of the Sanhedrin and other forces that sought to impede the spread of the gospel. Jesus thus provided his disciples with comprehensive instruction regarding the Holy Spirit in advance, equipping them with the knowledge and guidance necessary to fulfill their mission with the assistance of the Holy Spirit. Subsequently, the disciples of Jesus would be subjected to trials by the Sanhedrin, expelled from Judaism, and ultimately martyred for their adherence to the teachings of Jesus. This is evidenced by the confessions of the Apostle Paul, who was previously an adversary of the early Christian movement.

"For you have heard of my previous way of life in Judaism,
how intensely I persecuted the church of God and tried to destroy it.
I was advancing in Judaism beyond many of my own age among
my people and was extremely zealous for the traditions of my fathers."
(Galatians 1:13-14)

"I too was convinced that I ought to do all that was possible to oppose the name of Jesus of Nazareth.
And that is just what I did in Jerusalem.
On the authority of the chief priests I put many of the Lord's people in prison, and when they were put to death, I cast my vote against them.
Many a time I went from one synagogue to another to have them punished, and I tried to force them to blaspheme.
I was so obsessed with persecuting them that I even hunted them down in foreign cities." (Acts 26:9-11)

Upon Jesus' introduction of the Holy Spirit to his disciples, foreshadowing his impending suffering, they were too intimidated to inquire about his whereabouts (John 16:5-6). However, Jesus offers them further solace by promising the advent of the Comforter, the Holy Spirit, who will come to convict the world of sin, of righteousness, and of judgment.

The Holy Spirit works in the following ways.

The function of the Holy Spirit is to convict individuals of the sin of unbelief.

"about sin, because people do not believe in me." (John 16:9)

The Holy Spirit serves to reveal the righteousness of Christ as a genuine and authentic form of righteousness.

"About righteousness, because I am going to the Father,
where you can see me no longer." (John 16:10)

The Holy Spirit reveals that those who oppose Christ will be judged by God.

"And about judgment, because the prince of this world now stands condemned." (John 16:11).

Consequently, it will be through this same work of the Holy Spirit that people will be brought to repentance.

"When the people heard this,
they were cut to the heart and said to Peter and the other apostles,
"Brothers, what shall we do?"
Peter replied, "Repent and be baptized, every one of you, in the name of Jesus Christ for the forgiveness of your sins. And you will receive the gift of the Holy Spirit.

St. Peter preaching on Pentecost | Masolino da Panicale 作

The promise is for you and your children and for all who are far off—for all whom the Lord our God will call." (Acts 2:37-39)

In this way, Jesus encouraged his disciples, informing them that the Holy Spirit would assume control and provide guidance for his ministry.

Secondly, the Holy Spirit, also known as the Comforter, provides guidance to Christians on the path towards truth.

"I have much more to say to you,
more than you can now bear. But when he, the Spirit of truth, comes,
he will guide you into all the truth.
He will not speak on his own; he will speak only what he hears,
and he will tell you what is yet to come." (John 16:12-13)

Jesus answered, "I am the way and the truth and the life. No one comes to the Father except through me." (John 14:6). The Holy Spirit, also known as the Comforter, will provide guidance for us to live in a manner that aligns with the teachings of Jesus, who is regarded as the embodiment of truth and the path to spiritual enlightenment. The Holy Spirit of truth will facilitate our ability to live in accordance with the truth.

Thirdly, the Holy Spirit, also known as the Comforter, serves to bear witness to Jesus and to reveal His glory.

"He will glorify me because it is from me
that he will receive what he will make known to you.
All that belongs to the Father is mine.

That is why I said the Spirit will receive from me
what he will make known to you." (John 16:14-15)

In the same way that Jesus revealed the glory of God, the Holy Spirit will reveal the glory of Jesus. However, this has not yet occurred, as the Holy Spirit will only come after the crucifixion, resurrection, and ascension of Jesus.

"By this he meant the Spirit,
whom those who believed in him were later to receive.
Up to that time the Spirit had not been given,
since Jesus had not yet been glorified." (John 7:39)

The Holy Spirit, also known as the Comforter, will come and bear witness to all of Jesus' actions that were performed in accordance with the principles of righteousness. 'The first Eucharist, the prayer in the Garden of Gethsemane, the trial before the Sanhedrin, the trial before Pilate, the crucifixion, the resurrection, and the ascension.' This will serve to enhance the perception of Jesus' glory and elucidate the righteousness of Jesus. The Holy Spirit provides an accurate account of Jesus' ministry, precisely as it occurred, and guides us to offer an accurate account of Jesus' ministry, thereby revealing Jesus' glory. While the Holy Spirit may inspire joyous celebration, it is the accurate witness to the work of Jesus that the Holy Spirit finds most pleasing.

Furthermore, the Holy Spirit serves to reveal the glory of Jesus and to exalt Jesus. The salvific work of Jesus on the cross, the glory of Jesus, is revealed by the Holy Spirit.

The descent of the holy spirit | Anthony Van Dyck 作

Meanwhile, the Holy Spirit that Jesus had promised to send came upon the 120 people gathered in Mark's upper room on Pentecost, 50 days after Passover, not long after Jesus' ascension into heaven.

"When the day of Pentecost came, hey were all together in one place.
Suddenly a sound like the blowing of a violent wind came from heaven and filled the whole house where they were sitting.
They saw what seemed to be tongues of fire that separated
and came to rest on each of them.
All of them were filled with the Holy Spirit and began to speak
in other tongues as the Spirit enabled them." (Acts 2:1-4).

The reason the Holy Spirit came upon the disciples in the upper room and not the Jerusalem temple is that when Jesus said, "It is finished," on the cross of Calvary, the curtain of the Jerusalem temple was torn from top to bottom, thereby ending the function of the Jerusalem temple building. This event constituted a fulfillment of the Old Testament prophecies ascribed to Isaiah and Joel.

"Till the Spirit is poured on us from on high,
and the desert becomes a fertile field,
and the fertile field seems like a forest." (Isaiah 32:15)

"And afterward, I will pour out my Spirit on all people.
Your sons and daughters will prophesy,
your old men will dream dreams,
your young men will see visions.
Even on my servants, both men and women,

I will pour out my Spirit in those days.
I will show wonders in the heavens and on the earth,
blood and fire and billows of smoke." (Joel 2:28-30)

Upon the descent of the Holy Spirit upon the upper room of Mark, the Jews in the diaspora were astonished. The impact is further amplified by the fact that the Jews in the diaspora and Gentiles who had converted to Judaism were gathering in Jerusalem to celebrate Pentecost.

"Amazed and perplexed, they asked one another,
"What does this mean?"
Some, however, made fun of them and said,
"They have had too much wine." (Acts 2:12-13)

The Jews and Gentiles from the diaspora who had gathered in Jerusalem at that time observed for the first time the people of God filled with the Holy Spirit. The sight was so extraordinary that some suggested they were under the influence of a new intoxicant. The content of the tongues they spoke in other languages as the Holy Spirit caused them to speak was consistent with Peter's message, which was later recorded. This message served as a testament to Jesus' saving work and the great work of God (Acts 2:11).

"Then Peter stood up with the Eleven,
raised his voice and addressed the crowd:
"Fellow Jews and all of you who live in Jerusalem,
let me explain this to you; listen carefully to what I say.

These people are not drunk,
as you suppose. It's only nine in the morning!" (Acts 2:14-15)

The profound story of the Holy Spirit's presence as taught by Jesus should not be limited to the phenomenon that occurred at Pentecost. Rather, it should be understood as a continuous and ongoing presence, manifesting in various forms and contexts. It is imperative that the narrative of the Holy Spirit be conveyed with sincerity and gravity, commencing with Jesus' proclamation at the inaugural Eucharist prior to the descent of the Holy Spirit.

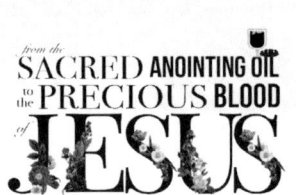

The Communion as a Mission of the Great Commission

The most comprehensive manual for humanity, created by the divine entity that is God, is the Creator's account of the seven days of creation. No subsequent manual has ever been able to surpass it. In six days, God created all things in the universe, rested on the seventh day, and blessed and sanctified that day. Subsequently, God established a kingdom of priests with the objective of bestowing blessings upon 'all nations.' The laws of this kingdom required that all individuals adhere to a 'weekly' manual, comprising six days of strenuous labor and a seventh day of rest.

The manual for resting on the Sabbath was not solely applicable to the Israelites, who were in a priestly covenant with God; it also extended to slaves, strangers, and all livestock. This was because God had established the Sabbath as a fundamental and indisputable tenet of the priestly law.

"Observe the Sabbath day by keeping it holy,
as the Lord your God has commanded you.
Six days you shall labor and do all your work,

but the seventh day is a sabbath to the Lord your God.
On it you shall not do any work, neither you, nor your son or daughter, nor your male or female servant, nor your ox,
your donkey or any of your animals,
nor any foreigner residing in your towns,
so that your male and female servants may rest, as you do."
(Deuteronomy 5:12-14)

However, the Lord's Supper, which commemorates the Lord's flesh and blood in bread and wine, is arguably the most significant manual of all. In place of the five sacrifices prescribed by the priestly system, Jesus instituted a single sacrifice on the cross. He also provided a manual for the celebration of the Eucharist, which serves as a guide for commemorating this singular act of sacrifice. In creating a communion manual, Jesus provided a means for the celebration of the flesh and blood of Jesus in bread and wine. Over the course of two millennia, innumerable individuals, both past and future, have utilized this manual to commemorate the cross of Jesus. Consequently, as members of the Christian community within the kingdom of God, we are privileged to partake in the sacred rite of communion, which bestows upon us a profound sense of joy and spiritual fulfilment.

The first communion of Jesus with his disciples gave rise to the subsequent commemoration and witness of Christians, who commemorated Jesus' death with bread and wine, bearing witness to the Lord's blood shed on the cross for all nations.

In his testimony, the Apostle Peter asserted that the precious blood of the Lamb, shed by Jesus, was the means of our redemption.

"But with the precious blood of Christ,
a lamb without blemish or defect." (1 Peter 1:19)

John, the younger brother of James, was the youngest of Jesus' twelve disciples. However, many years later, after the majority of the first generation of Jesus' disciples had been martyred, John was the sole survivor, becoming an adult in the church and assuming responsibility for caring for and leading the second generation. Subsequent to perusing the Gospels of Matthew, Mark, and Luke, as well as the previously documented testimonies of Jesus, the apostle John, with the assistance of the Holy Spirit, proceeded to compose five additional books, including the Gospel of John, I, II, and III John, and Revelation. In the Gospel of John, the author provides a substantial amount of significant information about Jesus' final week. This includes detailed accounts of Jesus' interactions with his disciples during the celebration of the Last Supper, which took place prior to his arrest by the Sanhedrin.

Additionally, the apostle John attested to the efficacy of Jesus' sacrifice, testifying to the 'blood of Jesus.'

"But if we walk in the light, as he is in the light,
we have fellowship with one another, and the blood of Jesus, his Son, purifies us from all sin." (1 John 1:7)

"And from Jesus Christ, who is the faithful witness,

the firstborn from the dead, and the ruler of the kings of the earth. To him who loves us and has freed us from our sins by his blood."
(Revelation 1:5)

The Apostle Paul performed the rite of baptism on members of the church in Rome and instructed members of the church in Corinth on the nature and significance of the sacraments. Paul instructed his followers in the sacraments of baptism and the Lord's Supper, as they were instituted by Jesus and bestowed upon the people of Jesus, who have become Christians. Baptism is performed with water, and the Lord's Supper is conducted with bread and wine. It is therefore incumbent upon us to be fully conversant with and to observe the sacraments as they were instituted by Jesus.

The 'Word of God' is comprised of three fundamental elements: God's grace, God's love, and God's blessings. These three elements, when considered collectively, form the basis of the 'Word of God." As previously stated, the "invisible word" is the word inscribed in the Bible. Indeed, at the outset, the Word of God was conveyed orally, without any written form. The written word of God is the Bible; thus, the written word is the 'invisible word.'

The 'visible word' is defined as the sacraments and baptism. Baptism is not merely a matter of words. Baptism necessitates the presence of water. The manner in which water is used in the rite of baptism—whether as a sprinkling or an immersion—may vary from time to time. However, the essential symbolism of water in baptism is that of cleansing and regeneration, signifying the washing away of sins and the beginning of a life of being a child of God.

At the inception of his ministry, Jesus initiated his disciples with the rite of baptism and subsequently exhorted them to perpetuate it (Matthew 28:19). Therefore, it is imperative that we do not alter or abandon the practice of baptism; rather, we must adhere to it and adhere to the teachings of Jesus.

Additionally, Jesus established the Lord's Supper as a sacrament. The Lord's Supper is a sacrament of the Christian faith, in which bread and wine are consumed as a symbol of the crucifixion of Jesus.

Baptism and the Lord's Supper are two visible signs of God's grace. They are holy ordinances and sacraments that Christians are obliged to observe. It is essential that they understand them accurately based on the biblical record. When the meaning of baptism and the Lord's Supper is understood from the Bible and the foundation of faith, hope, and love is established on that understanding, the Christian life is pleasing to God. When the two sacraments of baptism and the Lord's Supper are correctly understood, it is possible to exclaim, "The grace of God and the Word of God are now visible to us!"

Paul was fully cognizant of the nature of baptism, the word of grace that Jesus bestowed upon the faithful through the use of water, and the Lord's Supper, the word of grace that Jesus bestowed upon the faithful through the use of bread and wine. He taught these sacraments to the saints. Let us undertake a more detailed examination of Paul's teachings regarding baptism as they were conveyed to the members of the Roman church.

"Or don't you know that all of us who were baptized into Christ Jesus were baptized into his death?
We were therefore buried with him through baptism into death in order that, just as Christ was raised from the dead through the glory of the Father, we too may live a new life.
For if we have been united with him in a death like his, we will certainly also be united with him in a resurrection like his.
For we know that our old self was crucified with him so that the body ruled by sin might be done away with,
that we should no longer be slaves to sin— because anyone who has died has been set free from sin." (Romans 6:3-7)

This is Paul's teaching to the members of the Roman church regarding the nature of baptism. The text comprises four principal sections. The initial section establishes the doctrine of baptism as a rite of union with Jesus. Paul taught the Roman believers that baptism could not be performed without the name of Jesus. Upon confessing "Jesus is Lord" and undergoing baptism in accordance with the likeness of Jesus' death, one becomes crucified with him.", Paul makes the following confession: "I have been crucified with Christ and I no longer live, but Christ lives in me (Galatians 2:20). This confession can only be made by those who have undergone baptism in the name of Jesus.

Secondly, there is a strong connection between baptism and the sacrament. Paul attests that through baptism and the death of Jesus, one is buried with Jesus. If the act of consuming the bread and wine were an act performed independently of Jesus, there would be no rationale for the Lord's Supper, which is the ingestion of his flesh and the imbibing of his blood. This is why the Lord's Supper is reserved for those who believe that Jesus died on the cross to atone for our sins, and why it is only for those who have been baptized. Baptism is the initial rite, followed by the sacrament.

Thirdly, the doctrine of the resurrection. Following his death on the cross, Jesus was resurrected. The idea that we will also be resurrected is based on the premise that we will be united with him in the same likeness as his resurrection. Paul taught that the resurrection of Jesus Christ constituted the inaugural resurrection, and that all who believe in it will be resurrected with Jesus.

The fourth is justification, which can be defined as the process of becoming righteous. When the sinful self is crucified with Jesus, the sinful body is put to death, thus ending the bondage to sin and establishing freedom from sin and justification. Baptism is a sacrament that justifies the individual who partakes in it. This is done in remembrance of Jesus' death, as outlined in the Lord's Supper. Moreover, when individuals are baptized and partake of the Lord's Supper in faith in Jesus, they believe that they will die with Jesus on the cross and be resurrected like Jesus. In his teachings to the members of the Roman church, Paul espoused the doctrine that justification is attained through faith in the eternal life of the resurrection.

The following provides a more detailed examination of the sacrament of communion as taught by Paul to the Corinthian church members.

"And when he had given thanks, he broke it and said,
"This is my body, which is for you; do this in remembrance of me."
In the same way, after supper he took the cup, saying,
"This cup is the new covenant in my blood;
do this, whenever you drink it, in remembrance of me."
For whenever you eat this bread and drink this cup,
you proclaim the Lord's death until he comes." (1 Corinthians 11:24-26)

Upon gathering with his twelve disciples in an upper room to partake in the Passover meal, Jesus established the Lord's Supper as a ritual to be celebrated for the remainder of his life. This was done through the recital of a prayer of thanksgiving. He commenced his inaugural communion with a prayer of gratitude for his sacrifice.

In a gesture of gratitude, Jesus performed the miracle of the fivefold multiplication during the Great Commission. He engaged in an extended discourse with a multitude exceeding 5,000 individuals, elucidating the tenets of the kingdom of God. As the day drew to a close, the disciples observed that the location was inadequate for the large number of people in attendance and that the evening was approaching. They suggested that the multitude be dispersed and directed to their respective villages and towns to procure sustenance.

Subsequently, Jesus instructed his disciples to provide the multitude with sustenance. The disciples were perplexed and inquired, "Should we procure two hundred denarii of bread and provide nourishment for them?" And they responded, "We had five loaves and two fish." He proceeded to relate the sequence of events that had transpired.

Jesus invited the multitude to recline on the grass in groups of fifty and a hundred. After "Taking the five loaves and the two fish and looking up to heaven, he gave thanks" (Matthew 14:19), he proceeded to break the loaves, bestow them upon his disciples, and subsequently have them distributed to the people. The events of that day are referred to as the 'miracle of the five loaves and fishes,' and it is documented that Jesus also performed the miracle of the 'seven loaves and fishes.' In this way, Jesus performed a miracle of the 'visible word,' whereby he prayed thanksgiving, broke bread, and fed the people during the public feeding.

Similarly, the Eucharist was a miracle of the 'visible word' that Jesus performed on the final day of his three-year public ministry with his disciples. The day in question also marked the conclusion of a 1,500-year period of priestly rule in Israel, and Jesus' actions represented a distinctive form of observance.

Jesus and his disciples had already celebrated two Passovers together during Jesus' public ministry. Consequently, on the first day of the Feast of Unleavened Bread, after three years of public ministry, the disciples approached Jesus and inquired about the location for preparing the Passover food (Matthew 26:17). Jesus instructed them to "Go into the city to a certain man and tell him, 'The Teacher says: My appointed time is near. I am going to celebrate the Passover with my disciples at your house.'" (Matthew 26:18), and they did as Jesus had instructed. According to the Gospel of Luke, the disciples who were dispatched to prepare the Passover that day were Peter and John.

The third Passover celebrated by Jesus and his disciples was distinct from the first and second. Jesus indicated his desire to partake in the Passover with his disciples, yet he made it clear that he would not do so again until the kingdom of God was fully established. This signified the end of 1,500 years of Passover celebrations in a kingdom of priests.

Similarly, as he had previously taken the loaves and fishes and offered thanksgiving when he was sick, he proceeded to break the bread and declare, "This is my body, which is given for you; do this in remembrance of me," and he then took the cup of wine and stated, "This cup is the new covenant in my blood; do this in remembrance of me whenever you drink it." This is a notable example of a 'new covenant' declaration. In this declaration, Jesus was establishing the termination of the previous covenant, the Sinai covenant, and the inauguration of a new covenant. In this way, Jesus established the sacrament of the Lord's Supper by taking the bread and wine and saying, "Do this in remembrance of me." He also informed them that each time they consumed the bread and wine, they were to recall Jesus' death repeatedly until Jesus' return. In a letter, Paul elucidated this concept and conveyed it to the Corinthian church for their edification regarding the Lord's Supper.

Paul's teachings to the Corinthian church regarding the Lord's Supper can be distilled into four key points.

Firstly, Paul's teachings indicate that the Lord's Supper, as instituted by Jesus, represents the establishment of the 'new covenant.' The new covenant is built on the foundation of the old covenant, which spanned

1,500 years and was centered on the role of a kingdom of priests. It is a promise that remains constant and unchanging.

Secondly, he instructed that the sacrament of the New Covenant, established by the flesh and blood of Jesus, should be observed with the reminder of Jesus's teachings. Baptism, in which one confesses sins and professes faith in Jesus, is a singular occurrence. Repetition of this ritual is a transgression of the plan Jesus established for humanity. It is recommended that the sacrament be repeated in commemoration of Jesus, with the experience of baptism being recalled throughout the lifespan.

Thirdly, it was incumbent upon the faithful to proclaim the Lord's death each time they partook of the bread and cup, until the Second Coming. In other words, Paul taught that they were not only to be aware of and commemorate this fact, but also to participate in the "Great Commission" of disseminating the gospel to all nations until Jesus's return. This commission was commemorated through the sacraments.

Fourthly, the literal fulfillment of the Great Commission, "until he comes," and the sacrament of the Lord's Supper, conclude with the return of Jesus.

It is reasonable to posit that the members of the Corinthian church were gratified by the receipt of Paul's letter, as were the members of the Roman church. These individuals were undoubtedly pleased to experience the joy of being a Christian, as well as the remarkable grace associated with baptism and the Lord's Supper.

The books of Acts through Revelation serve as testimonies to Jesus' declaration. It is incumbent upon every Christian, in the manner of Peter, John, and Paul, to bear witness to Jesus' inaugural declaration of the Lord's Supper. One might inquire as to the duration of this period. It is incumbent upon every Christian to bear witness until Jesus returns. The Great Commission of Jesus and the testimony of those who carry it out are inextricably linked. The Great Commission of Jesus should serve as the basis for our collective testimony. As we engage in the sacrament, Christians are called to embody the three declarations made by Jesus during the sacrament.

The celebration of the Eucharist is no longer confined to a specific location or date. It can be celebrated and the grace of God towards humanity can be witnessed at any time and in any place. Furthermore, the Eucharist facilitates the establishment of significant interpersonal connections.

One becomes a Christian through the act of baptism, whereby one is united with Jesus Christ through faith. Furthermore, the celebration of the Lord's Supper serves to establish a bond of fraternity and kinship with other believers, as they partake of the same flesh and blood of Christ. In the absence of a manual for the sacrament, it is unclear how Christians might live as brothers and sisters in Christ.

The sacrament of the Lord's Supper enables the full realization and celebration of the grace of Jesus' work of redemption for humanity. The commitment of Jesus' obedience to the cross is the foundation upon which Christianity is built, and it is through this that Christians are able

Ascension Of Christ | Robert wilhelm Ekman 作

to live a life of faith, hope, and love. A comprehensive understanding of the three declarations made by Jesus at his first communion, as recorded, enables one to approach the Lord's Supper with a heightened sense of reverence and to share the words "Remember me" with all Christians.

Upon reading the Bible for the first time and partaking of the sacrament, one may experience a certain degree of emotional response. However, upon repeating this process of reading, studying, and partaking, the emotional impact may be amplified. As this sense of the gospel grows, Christians will be impelled to see more of their fellow believers fulfilling Jesus' Great Commission each time they partake in the sacrament. We will fulfill our mission as Jesus' witnesses, with the hope that an increasing number of people will be invited to partake of the grace that leads us to become a kingdom and priests.

"But you will receive power when the Holy Spirit comes on you;
and you will be my witnesses in Jerusalem,
and in all Judea and Samaria, and to the ends of the earth." (Acts 1:8)

The mission of witness, as outlined in the Great Commission, was entrusted to us by Jesus Christ following his ascension into heaven. The Comforter, also known as the Holy Spirit, is with us at all times until Jesus' second coming.